# CRYPTO
# CURRENCY
# TRADING TRACKER

This book belongs to:

_____

_____

_____

# CRYPTO CURRENCY TRADING TRACKER

| Buy | Sell | Date Time | | Date Time | | Outcome |
|-----|------|-----------|--|-----------|--|---------|
| Pair | | Entry Price | | Exit Price | | Profit / Loss |

| Setup | | | | | | |
|-------|--|--|--|--|--|--|

| Mental State | | Exit Condition | |
|--------------|--|----------------|--|

| Notes: | | | | | | |
|--------|--|--|--|--|--|--|

| Satoshis W/L | | % of acct | | USD Value | |
|--------------|--|-----------|--|-----------|--|

| Buy | Sell | Date Time | | Date Time | | Outcome |
|-----|------|-----------|--|-----------|--|---------|
| Pair | | Entry Price | | Exit Price | | Profit / Loss |

| Setup | | | | | | |
|-------|--|--|--|--|--|--|

| Mental State | | Exit Condition | |
|--------------|--|----------------|--|

| Notes: | | | | | | |
|--------|--|--|--|--|--|--|

| Satoshis W/L | | % of acct | | USD Value | |
|--------------|--|-----------|--|-----------|--|

| Buy | Sell | Date Time | | Date Time | | Outcome |
|-----|------|-----------|--|-----------|--|---------|
| Pair | | Entry Price | | Exit Price | | Profit / Loss |

| Setup | | | | | | |
|-------|--|--|--|--|--|--|

| Mental State | | Exit Condition | |
|--------------|--|----------------|--|

| Notes: | | | | | | |
|--------|--|--|--|--|--|--|

| Satoshis W/L | | % of acct | | USD Value | |
|--------------|--|-----------|--|-----------|--|

# CRYPTO CURRENCY TRADING TRACKER

| Buy | Sell | Date Time | | Date Time | | Outcome |
|---|---|---|---|---|---|---|
| Pair | | Entry Price | | Exit Price | | Profit / Loss |

| Setup |
|---|

| Mental State | Exit Condition |
|---|---|

| Notes: |
|---|

| Satoshis W/L | | % of acct | | USD Value | |
|---|---|---|---|---|---|

| Buy | Sell | Date Time | | Date Time | | Outcome |
|---|---|---|---|---|---|---|
| Pair | | Entry Price | | Exit Price | | Profit / Loss |

| Setup |
|---|

| Mental State | Exit Condition |
|---|---|

| Notes: |
|---|

| Satoshis W/L | | % of acct | | USD Value | |
|---|---|---|---|---|---|

| Buy | Sell | Date Time | | Date Time | | Outcome |
|---|---|---|---|---|---|---|
| Pair | | Entry Price | | Exit Price | | Profit / Loss |

| Setup |
|---|

| Mental State | Exit Condition |
|---|---|

| Notes: |
|---|

| Satoshis W/L | | % of acct | | USD Value | |
|---|---|---|---|---|---|

# CRYPTO CURRENCY TRADING TRACKER

| Buy | Sell | Date Time | | Date Time | | Outcome |
|---|---|---|---|---|---|---|
| Pair | | Entry Price | | Exit Price | | Profit / Loss |

| Setup | | | | | | |
|---|---|---|---|---|---|---|
| Mental State | | | Exit Condition | | | |
| Notes: | | | | | | |
| Satoshis W/L | | % of acct | | USD Value | | |

| Buy | Sell | Date Time | | Date Time | | Outcome |
|---|---|---|---|---|---|---|
| Pair | | Entry Price | | Exit Price | | Profit / Loss |

| Setup | | | | | | |
|---|---|---|---|---|---|---|
| Mental State | | | Exit Condition | | | |
| Notes: | | | | | | |
| Satoshis W/L | | % of acct | | USD Value | | |

| Buy | Sell | Date Time | | Date Time | | Outcome |
|---|---|---|---|---|---|---|
| Pair | | Entry Price | | Exit Price | | Profit / Loss |

| Setup | | | | | | |
|---|---|---|---|---|---|---|
| Mental State | | | Exit Condition | | | |
| Notes: | | | | | | |
| Satoshis W/L | | % of acct | | USD Value | | |

# CRYPTO CURRENCY TRADING TRACKER

| Buy | Sell | Date Time | | Date Time | | Outcome |
|-----|------|-----------|--|-----------|--|---------|
| Pair | | Entry Price | | Exit Price | | Profit / Loss |

| Setup | | | | | | |
|-------|--|--|--|--|--|--|

| Mental State | | | Exit Condition | | | |
|--------------|--|--|----------------|--|--|--|

| Notes: | | | | | | |
|--------|--|--|--|--|--|--|

| Satoshis W/L | | % of acct | | USD Value | |
|--------------|--|-----------|--|-----------|--|

| Buy | Sell | Date Time | | Date Time | | Outcome |
|-----|------|-----------|--|-----------|--|---------|
| Pair | | Entry Price | | Exit Price | | Profit / Loss |

| Setup | | | | | | |
|-------|--|--|--|--|--|--|

| Mental State | | | Exit Condition | | | |
|--------------|--|--|----------------|--|--|--|

| Notes: | | | | | | |
|--------|--|--|--|--|--|--|

| Satoshis W/L | | % of acct | | USD Value | |
|--------------|--|-----------|--|-----------|--|

| Buy | Sell | Date Time | | Date Time | | Outcome |
|-----|------|-----------|--|-----------|--|---------|
| Pair | | Entry Price | | Exit Price | | Profit / Loss |

| Setup | | | | | | |
|-------|--|--|--|--|--|--|

| Mental State | | | Exit Condition | | | |
|--------------|--|--|----------------|--|--|--|

| Notes: | | | | | | |
|--------|--|--|--|--|--|--|

| Satoshis W/L | | % of acct | | USD Value | |
|--------------|--|-----------|--|-----------|--|

# CRYPTO CURRENCY TRADING TRACKER

| Buy | Sell | Date Time | | Date Time | | Outcome |
|---|---|---|---|---|---|---|
| Pair | | Entry Price | | Exit Price | | Profit / Loss |

**Setup**

| Mental State | Exit Condition |
|---|---|
| | |

**Notes:**

| Satoshis W/L | | % of acct | | USD Value | |
|---|---|---|---|---|---|

| Buy | Sell | Date Time | | Date Time | | Outcome |
|---|---|---|---|---|---|---|
| Pair | | Entry Price | | Exit Price | | Profit / Loss |

**Setup**

| Mental State | Exit Condition |
|---|---|
| | |

**Notes:**

| Satoshis W/L | | % of acct | | USD Value | |
|---|---|---|---|---|---|

| Buy | Sell | Date Time | | Date Time | | Outcome |
|---|---|---|---|---|---|---|
| Pair | | Entry Price | | Exit Price | | Profit / Loss |

**Setup**

| Mental State | Exit Condition |
|---|---|
| | |

**Notes:**

| Satoshis W/L | | % of acct | | USD Value | |
|---|---|---|---|---|---|

# CRYPTO CURRENCY TRADING TRACKER

| Buy | Sell | Date Time | | Date Time | | Outcome |
|-----|------|-----------|--|-----------|--|---------|
| Pair | | Entry Price | | Exit Price | | Profit / Loss |

| Setup |
|-------|
| |

| Mental State | Exit Condition |
|--------------|----------------|
| | |

| Notes: |
|--------|
| |

| Satoshis W/L | | % of acct | | USD Value | |
|--------------|--|-----------|--|-----------|--|

| Buy | Sell | Date Time | | Date Time | | Outcome |
|-----|------|-----------|--|-----------|--|---------|
| Pair | | Entry Price | | Exit Price | | Profit / Loss |

| Setup |
|-------|
| |

| Mental State | Exit Condition |
|--------------|----------------|
| | |

| Notes: |
|--------|
| |

| Satoshis W/L | | % of acct | | USD Value | |
|--------------|--|-----------|--|-----------|--|

| Buy | Sell | Date Time | | Date Time | | Outcome |
|-----|------|-----------|--|-----------|--|---------|
| Pair | | Entry Price | | Exit Price | | Profit / Loss |

| Setup |
|-------|
| |

| Mental State | Exit Condition |
|--------------|----------------|
| | |

| Notes: |
|--------|
| |

| Satoshis W/L | | % of acct | | USD Value | |
|--------------|--|-----------|--|-----------|--|

# CRYPTO CURRENCY TRADING TRACKER

| Buy | Sell | Date Time | | Date Time | | Outcome |
|-----|------|-----------|--|-----------|--|---------|
| Pair | | Entry Price | | Exit Price | | Profit / Loss |

| Setup | | | | | | |
|-------|--|--|--|--|--|--|

| Mental State | | | Exit Condition | | | |
|--------------|--|--|----------------|--|--|--|

| Notes: | | | | | | |
|--------|--|--|--|--|--|--|

| Satoshis W/L | | % of acct | | USD Value | |
|--------------|--|-----------|--|-----------|--|

| Buy | Sell | Date Time | | Date Time | | Outcome |
|-----|------|-----------|--|-----------|--|---------|
| Pair | | Entry Price | | Exit Price | | Profit / Loss |

| Setup | | | | | | |
|-------|--|--|--|--|--|--|

| Mental State | | | Exit Condition | | | |
|--------------|--|--|----------------|--|--|--|

| Notes: | | | | | | |
|--------|--|--|--|--|--|--|

| Satoshis W/L | | % of acct | | USD Value | |
|--------------|--|-----------|--|-----------|--|

| Buy | Sell | Date Time | | Date Time | | Outcome |
|-----|------|-----------|--|-----------|--|---------|
| Pair | | Entry Price | | Exit Price | | Profit / Loss |

| Setup | | | | | | |
|-------|--|--|--|--|--|--|

| Mental State | | | Exit Condition | | | |
|--------------|--|--|----------------|--|--|--|

| Notes: | | | | | | |
|--------|--|--|--|--|--|--|

| Satoshis W/L | | % of acct | | USD Value | |
|--------------|--|-----------|--|-----------|--|

# CRYPTO CURRENCY TRADING TRACKER

| Buy | Sell | Date Time | | Date Time | | Outcome |
|---|---|---|---|---|---|---|
| Pair | | Entry Price | | Exit Price | | Profit / Loss |

| Setup | | | | | | |
|---|---|---|---|---|---|---|

| Mental State | | | Exit Condition | | | |
|---|---|---|---|---|---|---|

| Notes: | | | | | | |
|---|---|---|---|---|---|---|

| Satoshis W/L | | % of acct | | USD Value | |
|---|---|---|---|---|---|

| Buy | Sell | Date Time | | Date Time | | Outcome |
|---|---|---|---|---|---|---|
| Pair | | Entry Price | | Exit Price | | Profit / Loss |

| Setup | | | | | | |
|---|---|---|---|---|---|---|

| Mental State | | | Exit Condition | | | |
|---|---|---|---|---|---|---|

| Notes: | | | | | | |
|---|---|---|---|---|---|---|

| Satoshis W/L | | % of acct | | USD Value | |
|---|---|---|---|---|---|

| Buy | Sell | Date Time | | Date Time | | Outcome |
|---|---|---|---|---|---|---|
| Pair | | Entry Price | | Exit Price | | Profit / Loss |

| Setup | | | | | | |
|---|---|---|---|---|---|---|

| Mental State | | | Exit Condition | | | |
|---|---|---|---|---|---|---|

| Notes: | | | | | | |
|---|---|---|---|---|---|---|

| Satoshis W/L | | % of acct | | USD Value | |
|---|---|---|---|---|---|

# CRYPTO CURRENCY TRADING TRACKER

| Buy | Sell | Date Time | | Date Time | | Outcome |
|---|---|---|---|---|---|---|
| Pair | | Entry Price | | Exit Price | | Profit / Loss |

| Setup | | | |
|---|---|---|---|
| Mental State | | Exit Condition | |
| Notes: | | | |
| Satoshis W/L | | % of acct | | USD Value | |

| Buy | Sell | Date Time | | Date Time | | Outcome |
|---|---|---|---|---|---|---|
| Pair | | Entry Price | | Exit Price | | Profit / Loss |

| Setup | | | |
|---|---|---|---|
| Mental State | | Exit Condition | |
| Notes: | | | |
| Satoshis W/L | | % of acct | | USD Value | |

| Buy | Sell | Date Time | | Date Time | | Outcome |
|---|---|---|---|---|---|---|
| Pair | | Entry Price | | Exit Price | | Profit / Loss |

| Setup | | | |
|---|---|---|---|
| Mental State | | Exit Condition | |
| Notes: | | | |
| Satoshis W/L | | % of acct | | USD Value | |

# CRYPTO CURRENCY TRADING TRACKER

| Buy | Sell | Date Time | | Date Time | | Outcome |
|---|---|---|---|---|---|---|
| Pair | | Entry Price | | Exit Price | | Profit / Loss |

| Setup | | |
|---|---|---|
| Mental State | Exit Condition | |
| Notes: | | |
| Satoshis W/L | | % of acct | | USD Value | |

| Buy | Sell | Date Time | | Date Time | | Outcome |
|---|---|---|---|---|---|---|
| Pair | | Entry Price | | Exit Price | | Profit / Loss |

| Setup | | |
|---|---|---|
| Mental State | Exit Condition | |
| Notes: | | |
| Satoshis W/L | | % of acct | | USD Value | |

| Buy | Sell | Date Time | | Date Time | | Outcome |
|---|---|---|---|---|---|---|
| Pair | | Entry Price | | Exit Price | | Profit / Loss |

| Setup | | |
|---|---|---|
| Mental State | Exit Condition | |
| Notes: | | |
| Satoshis W/L | | % of acct | | USD Value | |

# CRYPTO CURRENCY TRADING TRACKER

| Buy | Sell | Date Time | | Date Time | | Outcome |
|---|---|---|---|---|---|---|
| Pair | | Entry Price | | Exit Price | | Profit / Loss |

| Setup |
|---|

| Mental State | Exit Condition |
|---|---|

| Notes: |
|---|

| Satoshis W/L | | % of acct | | USD Value | |
|---|---|---|---|---|---|

| Buy | Sell | Date Time | | Date Time | | Outcome |
|---|---|---|---|---|---|---|
| Pair | | Entry Price | | Exit Price | | Profit / Loss |

| Setup |
|---|

| Mental State | Exit Condition |
|---|---|

| Notes: |
|---|

| Satoshis W/L | | % of acct | | USD Value | |
|---|---|---|---|---|---|

| Buy | Sell | Date Time | | Date Time | | Outcome |
|---|---|---|---|---|---|---|
| Pair | | Entry Price | | Exit Price | | Profit / Loss |

| Setup |
|---|

| Mental State | Exit Condition |
|---|---|

| Notes: |
|---|

| Satoshis W/L | | % of acct | | USD Value | |
|---|---|---|---|---|---|

# CRYPTO CURRENCY TRADING TRACKER

| Buy | Sell | Date Time | | Date Time | | Outcome |
|-----|------|-----------|---|-----------|---|---------|
| Pair | | Entry Price | | Exit Price | | Profit / Loss |

**Setup**

| Mental State | Exit Condition |
|--------------|----------------|
| | |

**Notes:**

| Satoshis W/L | | % of acct | | USD Value | |
|--------------|---|-----------|---|-----------|---|

| Buy | Sell | Date Time | | Date Time | | Outcome |
|-----|------|-----------|---|-----------|---|---------|
| Pair | | Entry Price | | Exit Price | | Profit / Loss |

**Setup**

| Mental State | Exit Condition |
|--------------|----------------|
| | |

**Notes:**

| Satoshis W/L | | % of acct | | USD Value | |
|--------------|---|-----------|---|-----------|---|

| Buy | Sell | Date Time | | Date Time | | Outcome |
|-----|------|-----------|---|-----------|---|---------|
| Pair | | Entry Price | | Exit Price | | Profit / Loss |

**Setup**

| Mental State | Exit Condition |
|--------------|----------------|
| | |

**Notes:**

| Satoshis W/L | | % of acct | | USD Value | |
|--------------|---|-----------|---|-----------|---|

# CRYPTO CURRENCY TRADING TRACKER

| Buy | Sell | Date Time | | Date Time | | Outcome | |
|---|---|---|---|---|---|---|---|
| Pair | | Entry Price | | Exit Price | | Profit / Loss | |

**Setup**

| Mental State | Exit Condition |
|---|---|
| | |

**Notes:**

| Satoshis W/L | | % of acct | | USD Value | |
|---|---|---|---|---|---|

| Buy | Sell | Date Time | | Date Time | | Outcome | |
|---|---|---|---|---|---|---|---|
| Pair | | Entry Price | | Exit Price | | Profit / Loss | |

**Setup**

| Mental State | Exit Condition |
|---|---|
| | |

**Notes:**

| Satoshis W/L | | % of acct | | USD Value | |
|---|---|---|---|---|---|

| Buy | Sell | Date Time | | Date Time | | Outcome | |
|---|---|---|---|---|---|---|---|
| Pair | | Entry Price | | Exit Price | | Profit / Loss | |

**Setup**

| Mental State | Exit Condition |
|---|---|
| | |

**Notes:**

| Satoshis W/L | | % of acct | | USD Value | |
|---|---|---|---|---|---|

# CRYPTO CURRENCY TRADING TRACKER

| Buy | Sell | Date Time | | Date Time | | Outcome |
|---|---|---|---|---|---|---|
| Pair | | Entry Price | | Exit Price | | Profit / Loss |

| Setup | | | | | | |
|---|---|---|---|---|---|---|

| Mental State | | | Exit Condition | | | |
|---|---|---|---|---|---|---|

| Notes: | | | | | | |
|---|---|---|---|---|---|---|

| Satoshis W/L | | | % of acct | | USD Value | |
|---|---|---|---|---|---|---|

| Buy | Sell | Date Time | | Date Time | | Outcome |
|---|---|---|---|---|---|---|
| Pair | | Entry Price | | Exit Price | | Profit / Loss |

| Setup | | | | | | |
|---|---|---|---|---|---|---|

| Mental State | | | Exit Condition | | | |
|---|---|---|---|---|---|---|

| Notes: | | | | | | |
|---|---|---|---|---|---|---|

| Satoshis W/L | | | % of acct | | USD Value | |
|---|---|---|---|---|---|---|

| Buy | Sell | Date Time | | Date Time | | Outcome |
|---|---|---|---|---|---|---|
| Pair | | Entry Price | | Exit Price | | Profit / Loss |

| Setup | | | | | | |
|---|---|---|---|---|---|---|

| Mental State | | | Exit Condition | | | |
|---|---|---|---|---|---|---|

| Notes: | | | | | | |
|---|---|---|---|---|---|---|

| Satoshis W/L | | | % of acct | | USD Value | |
|---|---|---|---|---|---|---|

# CRYPTO CURRENCY TRADING TRACKER

| Buy | Sell | Date Time | | Date Time | | Outcome |
|-----|------|-----------|---|-----------|---|---------|
| Pair | | Entry Price | | Exit Price | | Profit / Loss |

| Setup | | | | | | |
|-------|---|---|---|---|---|---|

| Mental State | Exit Condition |
|--------------|----------------|

| Notes: | | |
|--------|---|---|

| Satoshis W/L | | % of acct | | USD Value | |
|--------------|---|-----------|---|-----------|---|

| Buy | Sell | Date Time | | Date Time | | Outcome |
|-----|------|-----------|---|-----------|---|---------|
| Pair | | Entry Price | | Exit Price | | Profit / Loss |

| Setup | | | | | | |
|-------|---|---|---|---|---|---|

| Mental State | Exit Condition |
|--------------|----------------|

| Notes: | | |
|--------|---|---|

| Satoshis W/L | | % of acct | | USD Value | |
|--------------|---|-----------|---|-----------|---|

| Buy | Sell | Date Time | | Date Time | | Outcome |
|-----|------|-----------|---|-----------|---|---------|
| Pair | | Entry Price | | Exit Price | | Profit / Loss |

| Setup | | | | | | |
|-------|---|---|---|---|---|---|

| Mental State | Exit Condition |
|--------------|----------------|

| Notes: | | |
|--------|---|---|

| Satoshis W/L | | % of acct | | USD Value | |
|--------------|---|-----------|---|-----------|---|

# CRYPTO CURRENCY TRADING TRACKER

| Buy | Sell | Date Time | | Date Time | | Outcome |
|---|---|---|---|---|---|---|
| Pair | | Entry Price | | Exit Price | | Profit / Loss |

| Setup |
|---|

| Mental State | Exit Condition |
|---|---|

| Notes: |
|---|

| Satoshis W/L | | % of acct | | USD Value | |
|---|---|---|---|---|---|

| Buy | Sell | Date Time | | Date Time | | Outcome |
|---|---|---|---|---|---|---|
| Pair | | Entry Price | | Exit Price | | Profit / Loss |

| Setup |
|---|

| Mental State | Exit Condition |
|---|---|

| Notes: |
|---|

| Satoshis W/L | | % of acct | | USD Value | |
|---|---|---|---|---|---|

| Buy | Sell | Date Time | | Date Time | | Outcome |
|---|---|---|---|---|---|---|
| Pair | | Entry Price | | Exit Price | | Profit / Loss |

| Setup |
|---|

| Mental State | Exit Condition |
|---|---|

| Notes: |
|---|

| Satoshis W/L | | % of acct | | USD Value | |
|---|---|---|---|---|---|

# CRYPTO CURRENCY TRADING TRACKER

| Buy | Sell | Date Time | | Date Time | | Outcome |
|---|---|---|---|---|---|---|
| Pair | | Entry Price | | Exit Price | | Profit / Loss |

**Setup**

| Mental State | Exit Condition |
|---|---|
| | |

**Notes:**

| Satoshis W/L | | % of acct | | USD Value | |
|---|---|---|---|---|---|

---

| Buy | Sell | Date Time | | Date Time | | Outcome |
|---|---|---|---|---|---|---|
| Pair | | Entry Price | | Exit Price | | Profit / Loss |

**Setup**

| Mental State | Exit Condition |
|---|---|
| | |

**Notes:**

| Satoshis W/L | | % of acct | | USD Value | |
|---|---|---|---|---|---|

---

| Buy | Sell | Date Time | | Date Time | | Outcome |
|---|---|---|---|---|---|---|
| Pair | | Entry Price | | Exit Price | | Profit / Loss |

**Setup**

| Mental State | Exit Condition |
|---|---|
| | |

**Notes:**

| Satoshis W/L | | % of acct | | USD Value | |
|---|---|---|---|---|---|

# CRYPTO CURRENCY TRADING TRACKER

| Buy | Sell | Date Time | | Date Time | | Outcome |
|-----|------|-----------|---|-----------|---|---------|
| Pair | | Entry Price | | Exit Price | | Profit / Loss |

Setup

| Mental State | Exit Condition |
|--------------|----------------|

Notes:

| Satoshis W/L | | % of acct | | USD Value | |
|--------------|---|-----------|---|-----------|---|

| Buy | Sell | Date Time | | Date Time | | Outcome |
|-----|------|-----------|---|-----------|---|---------|
| Pair | | Entry Price | | Exit Price | | Profit / Loss |

Setup

| Mental State | Exit Condition |
|--------------|----------------|

Notes:

| Satoshis W/L | | % of acct | | USD Value | |
|--------------|---|-----------|---|-----------|---|

| Buy | Sell | Date Time | | Date Time | | Outcome |
|-----|------|-----------|---|-----------|---|---------|
| Pair | | Entry Price | | Exit Price | | Profit / Loss |

Setup

| Mental State | Exit Condition |
|--------------|----------------|

Notes:

| Satoshis W/L | | % of acct | | USD Value | |
|--------------|---|-----------|---|-----------|---|

# CRYPTO CURRENCY TRADING TRACKER

| Buy | Sell | Date Time | | Date Time | | Outcome |
|-----|------|-----------|---|-----------|---|---------|
| Pair | | Entry Price | | Exit Price | | Profit / Loss |

**Setup**

| Mental State | Exit Condition |
|--------------|----------------|
| | |

**Notes:**

| Satoshis W/L | | % of acct | | USD Value | |
|--------------|---|-----------|---|-----------|---|

| Buy | Sell | Date Time | | Date Time | | Outcome |
|-----|------|-----------|---|-----------|---|---------|
| Pair | | Entry Price | | Exit Price | | Profit / Loss |

**Setup**

| Mental State | Exit Condition |
|--------------|----------------|
| | |

**Notes:**

| Satoshis W/L | | % of acct | | USD Value | |
|--------------|---|-----------|---|-----------|---|

| Buy | Sell | Date Time | | Date Time | | Outcome |
|-----|------|-----------|---|-----------|---|---------|
| Pair | | Entry Price | | Exit Price | | Profit / Loss |

**Setup**

| Mental State | Exit Condition |
|--------------|----------------|
| | |

**Notes:**

| Satoshis W/L | | % of acct | | USD Value | |
|--------------|---|-----------|---|-----------|---|

# CRYPTO CURRENCY TRADING TRACKER

| Buy | Sell | Date Time | | Date Time | | Outcome |
|-----|------|-----------|--|-----------|--|---------|
| Pair | | Entry Price | | Exit Price | | Profit / Loss |

**Setup**

| Mental State | Exit Condition |
|--------------|----------------|
| | |

**Notes:**

| Satoshis W/L | | % of acct | | USD Value | |
|--------------|--|-----------|--|-----------|--|

| Buy | Sell | Date Time | | Date Time | | Outcome |
|-----|------|-----------|--|-----------|--|---------|
| Pair | | Entry Price | | Exit Price | | Profit / Loss |

**Setup**

| Mental State | Exit Condition |
|--------------|----------------|
| | |

**Notes:**

| Satoshis W/L | | % of acct | | USD Value | |
|--------------|--|-----------|--|-----------|--|

| Buy | Sell | Date Time | | Date Time | | Outcome |
|-----|------|-----------|--|-----------|--|---------|
| Pair | | Entry Price | | Exit Price | | Profit / Loss |

**Setup**

| Mental State | Exit Condition |
|--------------|----------------|
| | |

**Notes:**

| Satoshis W/L | | % of acct | | USD Value | |
|--------------|--|-----------|--|-----------|--|

# CRYPTO CURRENCY TRADING TRACKER

| Buy | Sell | Date Time | | Date Time | | Outcome |
|---|---|---|---|---|---|---|
| Pair | | Entry Price | | Exit Price | | Profit / Loss |

**Setup**

| Mental State | Exit Condition |
|---|---|
| | |

**Notes:**

| Satoshis W/L | | % of acct | | USD Value | |
|---|---|---|---|---|---|

| Buy | Sell | Date Time | | Date Time | | Outcome |
|---|---|---|---|---|---|---|
| Pair | | Entry Price | | Exit Price | | Profit / Loss |

**Setup**

| Mental State | Exit Condition |
|---|---|
| | |

**Notes:**

| Satoshis W/L | | % of acct | | USD Value | |
|---|---|---|---|---|---|

| Buy | Sell | Date Time | | Date Time | | Outcome |
|---|---|---|---|---|---|---|
| Pair | | Entry Price | | Exit Price | | Profit / Loss |

**Setup**

| Mental State | Exit Condition |
|---|---|
| | |

**Notes:**

| Satoshis W/L | | % of acct | | USD Value | |
|---|---|---|---|---|---|

# CRYPTO CURRENCY TRADING TRACKER

| Buy | Sell | Date Time | | Date Time | | Outcome |
|-----|------|-----------|--|-----------|--|---------|
| Pair | | Entry Price | | Exit Price | | Profit / Loss |

**Setup**

| Mental State | Exit Condition |
|--------------|----------------|

**Notes:**

| Satoshis W/L | | % of acct | | USD Value | |
|--------------|--|-----------|--|-----------|--|

| Buy | Sell | Date Time | | Date Time | | Outcome |
|-----|------|-----------|--|-----------|--|---------|
| Pair | | Entry Price | | Exit Price | | Profit / Loss |

**Setup**

| Mental State | Exit Condition |
|--------------|----------------|

**Notes:**

| Satoshis W/L | | % of acct | | USD Value | |
|--------------|--|-----------|--|-----------|--|

| Buy | Sell | Date Time | | Date Time | | Outcome |
|-----|------|-----------|--|-----------|--|---------|
| Pair | | Entry Price | | Exit Price | | Profit / Loss |

**Setup**

| Mental State | Exit Condition |
|--------------|----------------|

**Notes:**

| Satoshis W/L | | % of acct | | USD Value | |
|--------------|--|-----------|--|-----------|--|

# CRYPTO CURRENCY TRADING TRACKER

| Buy | Sell | Date Time | | Date Time | | Outcome |
|-----|------|-----------|---|-----------|---|---------|
| Pair | | Entry Price | | Exit Price | | Profit / Loss |

**Setup**

| Mental State | Exit Condition |
|--------------|----------------|
| | |

**Notes:**

| Satoshis W/L | | % of acct | | USD Value | |
|--------------|---|-----------|---|-----------|---|

| Buy | Sell | Date Time | | Date Time | | Outcome |
|-----|------|-----------|---|-----------|---|---------|
| Pair | | Entry Price | | Exit Price | | Profit / Loss |

**Setup**

| Mental State | Exit Condition |
|--------------|----------------|
| | |

**Notes:**

| Satoshis W/L | | % of acct | | USD Value | |
|--------------|---|-----------|---|-----------|---|

| Buy | Sell | Date Time | | Date Time | | Outcome |
|-----|------|-----------|---|-----------|---|---------|
| Pair | | Entry Price | | Exit Price | | Profit / Loss |

**Setup**

| Mental State | Exit Condition |
|--------------|----------------|
| | |

**Notes:**

| Satoshis W/L | | % of acct | | USD Value | |
|--------------|---|-----------|---|-----------|---|

# CRYPTO CURRENCY TRADING TRACKER

| Buy | Sell | Date Time | | Date Time | | Outcome |
|-----|------|-----------|--|-----------|--|---------|
| Pair | | Entry Price | | Exit Price | | Profit / Loss |

Setup

| Mental State | Exit Condition |
|--------------|----------------|

Notes:

| Satoshis W/L | | % of acct | | USD Value | |
|--------------|--|-----------|--|-----------|--|

| Buy | Sell | Date Time | | Date Time | | Outcome |
|-----|------|-----------|--|-----------|--|---------|
| Pair | | Entry Price | | Exit Price | | Profit / Loss |

Setup

| Mental State | Exit Condition |
|--------------|----------------|

Notes:

| Satoshis W/L | | % of acct | | USD Value | |
|--------------|--|-----------|--|-----------|--|

| Buy | Sell | Date Time | | Date Time | | Outcome |
|-----|------|-----------|--|-----------|--|---------|
| Pair | | Entry Price | | Exit Price | | Profit / Loss |

Setup

| Mental State | Exit Condition |
|--------------|----------------|

Notes:

| Satoshis W/L | | % of acct | | USD Value | |
|--------------|--|-----------|--|-----------|--|

# CRYPTO CURRENCY TRADING TRACKER

| Buy | Sell | Date Time | | Date Time | | Outcome |
|-----|------|-----------|--|-----------|--|---------|
| Pair | | Entry Price | | Exit Price | | Profit / Loss |

**Setup**

| Mental State | Exit Condition |
|--------------|----------------|

**Notes:**

| Satoshis W/L | | % of acct | | USD Value | |
|--------------|--|-----------|--|-----------|--|

| Buy | Sell | Date Time | | Date Time | | Outcome |
|-----|------|-----------|--|-----------|--|---------|
| Pair | | Entry Price | | Exit Price | | Profit / Loss |

**Setup**

| Mental State | Exit Condition |
|--------------|----------------|

**Notes:**

| Satoshis W/L | | % of acct | | USD Value | |
|--------------|--|-----------|--|-----------|--|

| Buy | Sell | Date Time | | Date Time | | Outcome |
|-----|------|-----------|--|-----------|--|---------|
| Pair | | Entry Price | | Exit Price | | Profit / Loss |

**Setup**

| Mental State | Exit Condition |
|--------------|----------------|

**Notes:**

| Satoshis W/L | | % of acct | | USD Value | |
|--------------|--|-----------|--|-----------|--|

# CRYPTO CURRENCY TRADING TRACKER

| Buy | Sell | Date Time | | Date Time | | Outcome |
|---|---|---|---|---|---|---|
| Pair | | Entry Price | | Exit Price | | Profit / Loss |

**Setup**

| Mental State | Exit Condition |
|---|---|

**Notes:**

| Satoshis W/L | | % of acct | | USD Value | |
|---|---|---|---|---|---|

| Buy | Sell | Date Time | | Date Time | | Outcome |
|---|---|---|---|---|---|---|
| Pair | | Entry Price | | Exit Price | | Profit / Loss |

**Setup**

| Mental State | Exit Condition |
|---|---|

**Notes:**

| Satoshis W/L | | % of acct | | USD Value | |
|---|---|---|---|---|---|

| Buy | Sell | Date Time | | Date Time | | Outcome |
|---|---|---|---|---|---|---|
| Pair | | Entry Price | | Exit Price | | Profit / Loss |

**Setup**

| Mental State | Exit Condition |
|---|---|

**Notes:**

| Satoshis W/L | | % of acct | | USD Value | |
|---|---|---|---|---|---|

# CRYPTO CURRENCY TRADING TRACKER

| Buy | Sell | Date Time | | Date Time | | Outcome |
|-----|------|-----------|---|-----------|---|---------|
| Pair | | Entry Price | | Exit Price | | Profit / Loss |

**Setup**

| Mental State | Exit Condition |
|--------------|----------------|

**Notes:**

| Satoshis W/L | | % of acct | | USD Value | |
|--------------|---|-----------|---|-----------|---|

| Buy | Sell | Date Time | | Date Time | | Outcome |
|-----|------|-----------|---|-----------|---|---------|
| Pair | | Entry Price | | Exit Price | | Profit / Loss |

**Setup**

| Mental State | Exit Condition |
|--------------|----------------|

**Notes:**

| Satoshis W/L | | % of acct | | USD Value | |
|--------------|---|-----------|---|-----------|---|

| Buy | Sell | Date Time | | Date Time | | Outcome |
|-----|------|-----------|---|-----------|---|---------|
| Pair | | Entry Price | | Exit Price | | Profit / Loss |

**Setup**

| Mental State | Exit Condition |
|--------------|----------------|

**Notes:**

| Satoshis W/L | | % of acct | | USD Value | |
|--------------|---|-----------|---|-----------|---|

# CRYPTO CURRENCY TRADING TRACKER

| Buy | Sell | Date Time | | Date Time | | Outcome |
|-----|------|-----------|--|-----------|--|---------|
| Pair | | Entry Price | | Exit Price | | Profit / Loss |

**Setup**

| Mental State | Exit Condition |
|--------------|----------------|

**Notes:**

| Satoshis W/L | | % of acct | | USD Value | |
|--------------|--|-----------|--|-----------|--|

| Buy | Sell | Date Time | | Date Time | | Outcome |
|-----|------|-----------|--|-----------|--|---------|
| Pair | | Entry Price | | Exit Price | | Profit / Loss |

**Setup**

| Mental State | Exit Condition |
|--------------|----------------|

**Notes:**

| Satoshis W/L | | % of acct | | USD Value | |
|--------------|--|-----------|--|-----------|--|

| Buy | Sell | Date Time | | Date Time | | Outcome |
|-----|------|-----------|--|-----------|--|---------|
| Pair | | Entry Price | | Exit Price | | Profit / Loss |

**Setup**

| Mental State | Exit Condition |
|--------------|----------------|

**Notes:**

| Satoshis W/L | | % of acct | | USD Value | |
|--------------|--|-----------|--|-----------|--|

# CRYPTO CURRENCY TRADING TRACKER

| Buy | Sell | Date Time | | Date Time | | Outcome |
|---|---|---|---|---|---|---|
| Pair | | Entry Price | | Exit Price | | Profit / Loss |

**Setup**

| Mental State | Exit Condition |
|---|---|
| | |

**Notes:**

| Satoshis W/L | | % of acct | | USD Value | |
|---|---|---|---|---|---|

| Buy | Sell | Date Time | | Date Time | | Outcome |
|---|---|---|---|---|---|---|
| Pair | | Entry Price | | Exit Price | | Profit / Loss |

**Setup**

| Mental State | Exit Condition |
|---|---|
| | |

**Notes:**

| Satoshis W/L | | % of acct | | USD Value | |
|---|---|---|---|---|---|

| Buy | Sell | Date Time | | Date Time | | Outcome |
|---|---|---|---|---|---|---|
| Pair | | Entry Price | | Exit Price | | Profit / Loss |

**Setup**

| Mental State | Exit Condition |
|---|---|
| | |

**Notes:**

| Satoshis W/L | | % of acct | | USD Value | |
|---|---|---|---|---|---|

# CRYPTO CURRENCY TRADING TRACKER

| Buy | Sell | Date Time | | Date Time | | Outcome |
|-----|------|-----------|---|-----------|---|---------|
| Pair | | Entry Price | | Exit Price | | Profit / Loss |

| Setup | | | | | | |
|-------|---|---|---|---|---|---|

| Mental State | | | Exit Condition | | | |
|--------------|---|---|---------------|---|---|---|

| Notes: | | | | | | |
|--------|---|---|---|---|---|---|

| Satoshis W/L | | % of acct | | USD Value | |
|--------------|---|-----------|---|-----------|---|

| Buy | Sell | Date Time | | Date Time | | Outcome |
|-----|------|-----------|---|-----------|---|---------|
| Pair | | Entry Price | | Exit Price | | Profit / Loss |

| Setup | | | | | | |
|-------|---|---|---|---|---|---|

| Mental State | | | Exit Condition | | | |
|--------------|---|---|---------------|---|---|---|

| Notes: | | | | | | |
|--------|---|---|---|---|---|---|

| Satoshis W/L | | % of acct | | USD Value | |
|--------------|---|-----------|---|-----------|---|

| Buy | Sell | Date Time | | Date Time | | Outcome |
|-----|------|-----------|---|-----------|---|---------|
| Pair | | Entry Price | | Exit Price | | Profit / Loss |

| Setup | | | | | | |
|-------|---|---|---|---|---|---|

| Mental State | | | Exit Condition | | | |
|--------------|---|---|---------------|---|---|---|

| Notes: | | | | | | |
|--------|---|---|---|---|---|---|

| Satoshis W/L | | % of acct | | USD Value | |
|--------------|---|-----------|---|-----------|---|

# CRYPTO CURRENCY TRADING TRACKER

| Buy | Sell | Date Time | | Date Time | | Outcome |
|-----|------|-----------|--|-----------|--|---------|
| Pair | | Entry Price | | Exit Price | | Profit / Loss |

**Setup**

| Mental State | Exit Condition |
|--------------|----------------|
| | |

**Notes:**

| Satoshis W/L | | % of acct | | USD Value | |
|--------------|--|-----------|--|-----------|--|

---

| Buy | Sell | Date Time | | Date Time | | Outcome |
|-----|------|-----------|--|-----------|--|---------|
| Pair | | Entry Price | | Exit Price | | Profit / Loss |

**Setup**

| Mental State | Exit Condition |
|--------------|----------------|
| | |

**Notes:**

| Satoshis W/L | | % of acct | | USD Value | |
|--------------|--|-----------|--|-----------|--|

---

| Buy | Sell | Date Time | | Date Time | | Outcome |
|-----|------|-----------|--|-----------|--|---------|
| Pair | | Entry Price | | Exit Price | | Profit / Loss |

**Setup**

| Mental State | Exit Condition |
|--------------|----------------|
| | |

**Notes:**

| Satoshis W/L | | % of acct | | USD Value | |
|--------------|--|-----------|--|-----------|--|

# CRYPTO CURRENCY TRADING TRACKER

| Buy | Sell | Date Time | | Date Time | | Outcome |
|-----|------|-----------|--|-----------|--|---------|
| Pair | | Entry Price | | Exit Price | | Profit / Loss |

**Setup**

| Mental State | Exit Condition |
|--------------|----------------|
| | |

**Notes:**

| Satoshis W/L | | % of acct | | USD Value | |
|--------------|--|-----------|--|-----------|--|

| Buy | Sell | Date Time | | Date Time | | Outcome |
|-----|------|-----------|--|-----------|--|---------|
| Pair | | Entry Price | | Exit Price | | Profit / Loss |

**Setup**

| Mental State | Exit Condition |
|--------------|----------------|
| | |

**Notes:**

| Satoshis W/L | | % of acct | | USD Value | |
|--------------|--|-----------|--|-----------|--|

| Buy | Sell | Date Time | | Date Time | | Outcome |
|-----|------|-----------|--|-----------|--|---------|
| Pair | | Entry Price | | Exit Price | | Profit / Loss |

**Setup**

| Mental State | Exit Condition |
|--------------|----------------|
| | |

**Notes:**

| Satoshis W/L | | % of acct | | USD Value | |
|--------------|--|-----------|--|-----------|--|

# CRYPTO CURRENCY TRADING TRACKER

| Buy | Sell | Date Time | | Date Time | | Outcome |
|---|---|---|---|---|---|---|
| Pair | | Entry Price | | Exit Price | | Profit / Loss |

| Setup | | | | | | |
|---|---|---|---|---|---|---|

| Mental State | | | Exit Condition | | | |
|---|---|---|---|---|---|---|

| Notes: | | | | | | |
|---|---|---|---|---|---|---|

| Satoshis W/L | | | % of acct | | USD Value | |
|---|---|---|---|---|---|---|

| Buy | Sell | Date Time | | Date Time | | Outcome |
|---|---|---|---|---|---|---|
| Pair | | Entry Price | | Exit Price | | Profit / Loss |

| Setup | | | | | | |
|---|---|---|---|---|---|---|

| Mental State | | | Exit Condition | | | |
|---|---|---|---|---|---|---|

| Notes: | | | | | | |
|---|---|---|---|---|---|---|

| Satoshis W/L | | | % of acct | | USD Value | |
|---|---|---|---|---|---|---|

| Buy | Sell | Date Time | | Date Time | | Outcome |
|---|---|---|---|---|---|---|
| Pair | | Entry Price | | Exit Price | | Profit / Loss |

| Setup | | | | | | |
|---|---|---|---|---|---|---|

| Mental State | | | Exit Condition | | | |
|---|---|---|---|---|---|---|

| Notes: | | | | | | |
|---|---|---|---|---|---|---|

| Satoshis W/L | | | % of acct | | USD Value | |
|---|---|---|---|---|---|---|

# CRYPTO CURRENCY TRADING TRACKER

| Buy | Sell | Date Time | | Date Time | | Outcome |
|-----|------|-----------|---|-----------|---|---------|
| Pair | | Entry Price | | Exit Price | | Profit / Loss |

| Setup | | | | | | |
|-------|---|---|---|---|---|---|

| Mental State | | | Exit Condition | | | |
|--------------|---|---|----------------|---|---|---|

| Notes: | | | | | | |
|--------|---|---|---|---|---|---|

| Satoshis W/L | | | % of acct | | USD Value | |
|--------------|---|---|-----------|---|-----------|---|

| Buy | Sell | Date Time | | Date Time | | Outcome |
|-----|------|-----------|---|-----------|---|---------|
| Pair | | Entry Price | | Exit Price | | Profit / Loss |

| Setup | | | | | | |
|-------|---|---|---|---|---|---|

| Mental State | | | Exit Condition | | | |
|--------------|---|---|----------------|---|---|---|

| Notes: | | | | | | |
|--------|---|---|---|---|---|---|

| Satoshis W/L | | | % of acct | | USD Value | |
|--------------|---|---|-----------|---|-----------|---|

| Buy | Sell | Date Time | | Date Time | | Outcome |
|-----|------|-----------|---|-----------|---|---------|
| Pair | | Entry Price | | Exit Price | | Profit / Loss |

| Setup | | | | | | |
|-------|---|---|---|---|---|---|

| Mental State | | | Exit Condition | | | |
|--------------|---|---|----------------|---|---|---|

| Notes: | | | | | | |
|--------|---|---|---|---|---|---|

| Satoshis W/L | | | % of acct | | USD Value | |
|--------------|---|---|-----------|---|-----------|---|

# CRYPTO CURRENCY TRADING TRACKER

| Buy | Sell | Date Time | | Date Time | | Outcome |
|-----|------|-----------|---|-----------|---|---------|
| Pair | | Entry Price | | Exit Price | | Profit / Loss |

Setup

| Mental State | | Exit Condition | |
|---|---|---|---|

Notes:

| Satoshis W/L | | % of acct | | USD Value | |
|---|---|---|---|---|---|

| Buy | Sell | Date Time | | Date Time | | Outcome |
|-----|------|-----------|---|-----------|---|---------|
| Pair | | Entry Price | | Exit Price | | Profit / Loss |

Setup

| Mental State | | Exit Condition | |
|---|---|---|---|

Notes:

| Satoshis W/L | | % of acct | | USD Value | |
|---|---|---|---|---|---|

| Buy | Sell | Date Time | | Date Time | | Outcome |
|-----|------|-----------|---|-----------|---|---------|
| Pair | | Entry Price | | Exit Price | | Profit / Loss |

Setup

| Mental State | | Exit Condition | |
|---|---|---|---|

Notes:

| Satoshis W/L | | % of acct | | USD Value | |
|---|---|---|---|---|---|

# CRYPTO CURRENCY TRADING TRACKER

| Buy | Sell | Date Time | | Date Time | | Outcome |
|-----|------|-----------|---|-----------|---|---------|
| Pair | | Entry Price | | Exit Price | | Profit / Loss |

| Setup |
|-------|
| |

| Mental State | Exit Condition |
|--------------|----------------|
| | |

| Notes: |
|--------|
| |

| Satoshis W/L | | % of acct | | USD Value | |
|--------------|---|-----------|---|-----------|---|

| Buy | Sell | Date Time | | Date Time | | Outcome |
|-----|------|-----------|---|-----------|---|---------|
| Pair | | Entry Price | | Exit Price | | Profit / Loss |

| Setup |
|-------|
| |

| Mental State | Exit Condition |
|--------------|----------------|
| | |

| Notes: |
|--------|
| |

| Satoshis W/L | | % of acct | | USD Value | |
|--------------|---|-----------|---|-----------|---|

| Buy | Sell | Date Time | | Date Time | | Outcome |
|-----|------|-----------|---|-----------|---|---------|
| Pair | | Entry Price | | Exit Price | | Profit / Loss |

| Setup |
|-------|
| |

| Mental State | Exit Condition |
|--------------|----------------|
| | |

| Notes: |
|--------|
| |

| Satoshis W/L | | % of acct | | USD Value | |
|--------------|---|-----------|---|-----------|---|

# CRYPTO CURRENCY TRADING TRACKER

| Buy | Sell | Date Time | | Date Time | | Outcome |
|-----|------|-----------|--|-----------|--|---------|
| Pair | | Entry Price | | Exit Price | | Profit / Loss |

**Setup**

| Mental State | Exit Condition |
|--------------|----------------|
| | |

**Notes:**

| Satoshis W/L | | % of acct | | USD Value | |
|--------------|--|-----------|--|-----------|--|

| Buy | Sell | Date Time | | Date Time | | Outcome |
|-----|------|-----------|--|-----------|--|---------|
| Pair | | Entry Price | | Exit Price | | Profit / Loss |

**Setup**

| Mental State | Exit Condition |
|--------------|----------------|
| | |

**Notes:**

| Satoshis W/L | | % of acct | | USD Value | |
|--------------|--|-----------|--|-----------|--|

| Buy | Sell | Date Time | | Date Time | | Outcome |
|-----|------|-----------|--|-----------|--|---------|
| Pair | | Entry Price | | Exit Price | | Profit / Loss |

**Setup**

| Mental State | Exit Condition |
|--------------|----------------|
| | |

**Notes:**

| Satoshis W/L | | % of acct | | USD Value | |
|--------------|--|-----------|--|-----------|--|

# CRYPTO CURRENCY TRADING TRACKER

| Buy | Sell | Date Time | | Date Time | | Outcome |
|-----|------|-----------|---|-----------|---|---------|
| Pair | | Entry Price | | Exit Price | | Profit / Loss |

**Setup**

| Mental State | | Exit Condition | |
|--------------|---|----------------|---|

**Notes:**

| Satoshis W/L | | % of acct | | USD Value | |
|--------------|---|-----------|---|-----------|---|

| Buy | Sell | Date Time | | Date Time | | Outcome |
|-----|------|-----------|---|-----------|---|---------|
| Pair | | Entry Price | | Exit Price | | Profit / Loss |

**Setup**

| Mental State | | Exit Condition | |
|--------------|---|----------------|---|

**Notes:**

| Satoshis W/L | | % of acct | | USD Value | |
|--------------|---|-----------|---|-----------|---|

| Buy | Sell | Date Time | | Date Time | | Outcome |
|-----|------|-----------|---|-----------|---|---------|
| Pair | | Entry Price | | Exit Price | | Profit / Loss |

**Setup**

| Mental State | | Exit Condition | |
|--------------|---|----------------|---|

**Notes:**

| Satoshis W/L | | % of acct | | USD Value | |
|--------------|---|-----------|---|-----------|---|

# CRYPTO CURRENCY TRADING TRACKER

| Buy | Sell | Date Time | | Date Time | | Outcome | |
|---|---|---|---|---|---|---|---|
| Pair | | Entry Price | | Exit Price | | Profit / Loss | |

| Setup | |
|---|---|

| Mental State | Exit Condition |
|---|---|
| | |

| Notes: |
|---|
| |

| Satoshis W/L | | % of acct | | USD Value | |
|---|---|---|---|---|---|

| Buy | Sell | Date Time | | Date Time | | Outcome | |
|---|---|---|---|---|---|---|---|
| Pair | | Entry Price | | Exit Price | | Profit / Loss | |

| Setup | |
|---|---|

| Mental State | Exit Condition |
|---|---|
| | |

| Notes: |
|---|
| |

| Satoshis W/L | | % of acct | | USD Value | |
|---|---|---|---|---|---|

| Buy | Sell | Date Time | | Date Time | | Outcome | |
|---|---|---|---|---|---|---|---|
| Pair | | Entry Price | | Exit Price | | Profit / Loss | |

| Setup | |
|---|---|

| Mental State | Exit Condition |
|---|---|
| | |

| Notes: |
|---|
| |

| Satoshis W/L | | % of acct | | USD Value | |
|---|---|---|---|---|---|

# CRYPTO CURRENCY TRADING TRACKER

| Buy | Sell | Date Time | | Date Time | | Outcome |
|---|---|---|---|---|---|---|
| Pair | | Entry Price | | Exit Price | | Profit / Loss |

| Setup | |
|---|---|
| Mental State | Exit Condition |
| Notes: | |

| Satoshis W/L | | % of acct | | USD Value | |
|---|---|---|---|---|---|

| Buy | Sell | Date Time | | Date Time | | Outcome |
|---|---|---|---|---|---|---|
| Pair | | Entry Price | | Exit Price | | Profit / Loss |

| Setup | |
|---|---|
| Mental State | Exit Condition |
| Notes: | |

| Satoshis W/L | | % of acct | | USD Value | |
|---|---|---|---|---|---|

| Buy | Sell | Date Time | | Date Time | | Outcome |
|---|---|---|---|---|---|---|
| Pair | | Entry Price | | Exit Price | | Profit / Loss |

| Setup | |
|---|---|
| Mental State | Exit Condition |
| Notes: | |

| Satoshis W/L | | % of acct | | USD Value | |
|---|---|---|---|---|---|

# CRYPTO CURRENCY TRADING TRACKER

| Buy | Sell | Date Time | | Date Time | | Outcome |
|---|---|---|---|---|---|---|
| Pair | | Entry Price | | Exit Price | | Profit / Loss |

| Setup |
|---|

| Mental State | Exit Condition |
|---|---|
| | |

| Notes: |
|---|
| |

| Satoshis W/L | | % of acct | | USD Value | |
|---|---|---|---|---|---|

---

| Buy | Sell | Date Time | | Date Time | | Outcome |
|---|---|---|---|---|---|---|
| Pair | | Entry Price | | Exit Price | | Profit / Loss |

| Setup |
|---|

| Mental State | Exit Condition |
|---|---|
| | |

| Notes: |
|---|
| |

| Satoshis W/L | | % of acct | | USD Value | |
|---|---|---|---|---|---|

---

| Buy | Sell | Date Time | | Date Time | | Outcome |
|---|---|---|---|---|---|---|
| Pair | | Entry Price | | Exit Price | | Profit / Loss |

| Setup |
|---|

| Mental State | Exit Condition |
|---|---|
| | |

| Notes: |
|---|
| |

| Satoshis W/L | | % of acct | | USD Value | |
|---|---|---|---|---|---|

# CRYPTO CURRENCY TRADING TRACKER

| Buy | Sell | Date Time | | Date Time | | Outcome |
|-----|------|-----------|---|-----------|---|---------|
| Pair | | Entry Price | | Exit Price | | Profit / Loss |

**Setup**

| Mental State | Exit Condition |
|---|---|
| | |

**Notes:**

| Satoshis W/L | | % of acct | | USD Value | |
|---|---|---|---|---|---|

| Buy | Sell | Date Time | | Date Time | | Outcome |
|-----|------|-----------|---|-----------|---|---------|
| Pair | | Entry Price | | Exit Price | | Profit / Loss |

**Setup**

| Mental State | Exit Condition |
|---|---|
| | |

**Notes:**

| Satoshis W/L | | % of acct | | USD Value | |
|---|---|---|---|---|---|

| Buy | Sell | Date Time | | Date Time | | Outcome |
|-----|------|-----------|---|-----------|---|---------|
| Pair | | Entry Price | | Exit Price | | Profit / Loss |

**Setup**

| Mental State | Exit Condition |
|---|---|
| | |

**Notes:**

| Satoshis W/L | | % of acct | | USD Value | |
|---|---|---|---|---|---|

# CRYPTO CURRENCY TRADING TRACKER

| Buy | Sell | Date Time | | Date Time | | Outcome |
|---|---|---|---|---|---|---|
| Pair | | Entry Price | | Exit Price | | Profit / Loss |

| Setup |
|---|

| Mental State | Exit Condition |
|---|---|

| Notes: |
|---|

| Satoshis W/L | | % of acct | | USD Value | |
|---|---|---|---|---|---|

| Buy | Sell | Date Time | | Date Time | | Outcome |
|---|---|---|---|---|---|---|
| Pair | | Entry Price | | Exit Price | | Profit / Loss |

| Setup |
|---|

| Mental State | Exit Condition |
|---|---|

| Notes: |
|---|

| Satoshis W/L | | % of acct | | USD Value | |
|---|---|---|---|---|---|

| Buy | Sell | Date Time | | Date Time | | Outcome |
|---|---|---|---|---|---|---|
| Pair | | Entry Price | | Exit Price | | Profit / Loss |

| Setup |
|---|

| Mental State | Exit Condition |
|---|---|

| Notes: |
|---|

| Satoshis W/L | | % of acct | | USD Value | |
|---|---|---|---|---|---|

# CRYPTO CURRENCY TRADING TRACKER

| Buy | Sell | Date Time | | Date Time | | Outcome |
|-----|------|-----------|---|-----------|---|---------|
| Pair | | Entry Price | | Exit Price | | Profit / Loss |

| Setup | | | | | | |
|-------|---|---|---|---|---|---|
| Mental State | | | Exit Condition | | | |
| Notes: | | | | | | |
| Satoshis W/L | | % of acct | | USD Value | | |

| Buy | Sell | Date Time | | Date Time | | Outcome |
|-----|------|-----------|---|-----------|---|---------|
| Pair | | Entry Price | | Exit Price | | Profit / Loss |

| Setup | | | | | | |
|-------|---|---|---|---|---|---|
| Mental State | | | Exit Condition | | | |
| Notes: | | | | | | |
| Satoshis W/L | | % of acct | | USD Value | | |

| Buy | Sell | Date Time | | Date Time | | Outcome |
|-----|------|-----------|---|-----------|---|---------|
| Pair | | Entry Price | | Exit Price | | Profit / Loss |

| Setup | | | | | | |
|-------|---|---|---|---|---|---|
| Mental State | | | Exit Condition | | | |
| Notes: | | | | | | |
| Satoshis W/L | | % of acct | | USD Value | | |

# CRYPTO CURRENCY TRADING TRACKER

| Buy | Sell | Date Time | | Date Time | | Outcome | |
|-----|------|-----------|---|-----------|---|---------|---|
| Pair | | Entry Price | | Exit Price | | Profit / Loss | |

**Setup**

| Mental State | Exit Condition |
|--------------|----------------|
| | |

**Notes:**

| Satoshis W/L | | % of acct | | USD Value | |
|--------------|---|-----------|---|-----------|---|

| Buy | Sell | Date Time | | Date Time | | Outcome | |
|-----|------|-----------|---|-----------|---|---------|---|
| Pair | | Entry Price | | Exit Price | | Profit / Loss | |

**Setup**

| Mental State | Exit Condition |
|--------------|----------------|
| | |

**Notes:**

| Satoshis W/L | | % of acct | | USD Value | |
|--------------|---|-----------|---|-----------|---|

| Buy | Sell | Date Time | | Date Time | | Outcome | |
|-----|------|-----------|---|-----------|---|---------|---|
| Pair | | Entry Price | | Exit Price | | Profit / Loss | |

**Setup**

| Mental State | Exit Condition |
|--------------|----------------|
| | |

**Notes:**

| Satoshis W/L | | % of acct | | USD Value | |
|--------------|---|-----------|---|-----------|---|

# CRYPTO CURRENCY TRADING TRACKER

| Buy | Sell | Date Time | | Date Time | | Outcome |
|---|---|---|---|---|---|---|
| Pair | | Entry Price | | Exit Price | | Profit / Loss |
| Setup | | | | | | |
| Mental State | | | Exit Condition | | | |
| Notes: | | | | | | |
| Satoshis W/L | | % of acct | | USD Value | | |

| Buy | Sell | Date Time | | Date Time | | Outcome |
|---|---|---|---|---|---|---|
| Pair | | Entry Price | | Exit Price | | Profit / Loss |
| Setup | | | | | | |
| Mental State | | | Exit Condition | | | |
| Notes: | | | | | | |
| Satoshis W/L | | % of acct | | USD Value | | |

| Buy | Sell | Date Time | | Date Time | | Outcome |
|---|---|---|---|---|---|---|
| Pair | | Entry Price | | Exit Price | | Profit / Loss |
| Setup | | | | | | |
| Mental State | | | Exit Condition | | | |
| Notes: | | | | | | |
| Satoshis W/L | | % of acct | | USD Value | | |

# CRYPTO CURRENCY TRADING TRACKER

| Buy | Sell | Date Time | | Date Time | | Outcome |
|-----|------|-----------|---|-----------|---|---------|
| Pair | | Entry Price | | Exit Price | | Profit / Loss |

**Setup**

| Mental State | Exit Condition |
|--------------|----------------|
| | |

**Notes:**

| Satoshis W/L | | % of acct | | USD Value | |
|--------------|---|-----------|---|-----------|---|

| Buy | Sell | Date Time | | Date Time | | Outcome |
|-----|------|-----------|---|-----------|---|---------|
| Pair | | Entry Price | | Exit Price | | Profit / Loss |

**Setup**

| Mental State | Exit Condition |
|--------------|----------------|
| | |

**Notes:**

| Satoshis W/L | | % of acct | | USD Value | |
|--------------|---|-----------|---|-----------|---|

| Buy | Sell | Date Time | | Date Time | | Outcome |
|-----|------|-----------|---|-----------|---|---------|
| Pair | | Entry Price | | Exit Price | | Profit / Loss |

**Setup**

| Mental State | Exit Condition |
|--------------|----------------|
| | |

**Notes:**

| Satoshis W/L | | % of acct | | USD Value | |
|--------------|---|-----------|---|-----------|---|

# CRYPTO CURRENCY TRADING TRACKER

| Buy | Sell | Date Time | | Date Time | | Outcome |
|-----|------|-----------|---|-----------|---|---------|
| Pair | | Entry Price | | Exit Price | | Profit / Loss |

Setup

| Mental State | Exit Condition |
|--------------|----------------|

Notes:

| Satoshis W/L | | % of acct | | USD Value | |
|--------------|---|-----------|---|-----------|---|

| Buy | Sell | Date Time | | Date Time | | Outcome |
|-----|------|-----------|---|-----------|---|---------|
| Pair | | Entry Price | | Exit Price | | Profit / Loss |

Setup

| Mental State | Exit Condition |
|--------------|----------------|

Notes:

| Satoshis W/L | | % of acct | | USD Value | |
|--------------|---|-----------|---|-----------|---|

| Buy | Sell | Date Time | | Date Time | | Outcome |
|-----|------|-----------|---|-----------|---|---------|
| Pair | | Entry Price | | Exit Price | | Profit / Loss |

Setup

| Mental State | Exit Condition |
|--------------|----------------|

Notes:

| Satoshis W/L | | % of acct | | USD Value | |
|--------------|---|-----------|---|-----------|---|

# CRYPTO CURRENCY TRADING TRACKER

| Buy | Sell | Date Time | | Date Time | | Outcome |
|-----|------|-----------|--|-----------|--|---------|
| Pair | | Entry Price | | Exit Price | | Profit / Loss |

Setup

| Mental State | Exit Condition |
|--------------|----------------|
| | |

Notes:

| Satoshis W/L | | % of acct | | USD Value | |
|--------------|--|-----------|--|-----------|--|

| Buy | Sell | Date Time | | Date Time | | Outcome |
|-----|------|-----------|--|-----------|--|---------|
| Pair | | Entry Price | | Exit Price | | Profit / Loss |

Setup

| Mental State | Exit Condition |
|--------------|----------------|
| | |

Notes:

| Satoshis W/L | | % of acct | | USD Value | |
|--------------|--|-----------|--|-----------|--|

| Buy | Sell | Date Time | | Date Time | | Outcome |
|-----|------|-----------|--|-----------|--|---------|
| Pair | | Entry Price | | Exit Price | | Profit / Loss |

Setup

| Mental State | Exit Condition |
|--------------|----------------|
| | |

Notes:

| Satoshis W/L | | % of acct | | USD Value | |
|--------------|--|-----------|--|-----------|--|

# CRYPTO CURRENCY TRADING TRACKER

| Buy | Sell | Date Time | | Date Time | | Outcome |
|-----|------|-----------|---|-----------|---|---------|
| Pair | | Entry Price | | Exit Price | | Profit / Loss |

| Setup | |
|-------|--|

| Mental State | Exit Condition |
|--------------|----------------|

| Notes: | |
|--------|--|

| Satoshis W/L | | % of acct | | USD Value | |
|--------------|--|-----------|--|-----------|--|

| Buy | Sell | Date Time | | Date Time | | Outcome |
|-----|------|-----------|---|-----------|---|---------|
| Pair | | Entry Price | | Exit Price | | Profit / Loss |

| Setup | |
|-------|--|

| Mental State | Exit Condition |
|--------------|----------------|

| Notes: | |
|--------|--|

| Satoshis W/L | | % of acct | | USD Value | |
|--------------|--|-----------|--|-----------|--|

| Buy | Sell | Date Time | | Date Time | | Outcome |
|-----|------|-----------|---|-----------|---|---------|
| Pair | | Entry Price | | Exit Price | | Profit / Loss |

| Setup | |
|-------|--|

| Mental State | Exit Condition |
|--------------|----------------|

| Notes: | |
|--------|--|

| Satoshis W/L | | % of acct | | USD Value | |
|--------------|--|-----------|--|-----------|--|

# CRYPTO CURRENCY TRADING TRACKER

| Buy | Sell | Date Time | | Date Time | | Outcome |
|---|---|---|---|---|---|---|
| Pair | | Entry Price | | Exit Price | | Profit / Loss |

**Setup**

| Mental State | Exit Condition |
|---|---|
| | |

**Notes:**

| Satoshis W/L | | % of acct | | USD Value | |
|---|---|---|---|---|---|

| Buy | Sell | Date Time | | Date Time | | Outcome |
|---|---|---|---|---|---|---|
| Pair | | Entry Price | | Exit Price | | Profit / Loss |

**Setup**

| Mental State | Exit Condition |
|---|---|
| | |

**Notes:**

| Satoshis W/L | | % of acct | | USD Value | |
|---|---|---|---|---|---|

| Buy | Sell | Date Time | | Date Time | | Outcome |
|---|---|---|---|---|---|---|
| Pair | | Entry Price | | Exit Price | | Profit / Loss |

**Setup**

| Mental State | Exit Condition |
|---|---|
| | |

**Notes:**

| Satoshis W/L | | % of acct | | USD Value | |
|---|---|---|---|---|---|

# CRYPTO CURRENCY TRADING TRACKER

| Buy | Sell | Date Time | | Date Time | | Outcome |
|-----|------|-----------|---|-----------|---|---------|
| Pair | | Entry Price | | Exit Price | | Profit / Loss |

| Setup | | | | | | |
|-------|---|---|---|---|---|---|

| Mental State | Exit Condition |
|--------------|----------------|

| Notes: |
|--------|

| Satoshis W/L | | % of acct | | USD Value | |
|--------------|---|-----------|---|-----------|---|

| Buy | Sell | Date Time | | Date Time | | Outcome |
|-----|------|-----------|---|-----------|---|---------|
| Pair | | Entry Price | | Exit Price | | Profit / Loss |

| Setup | | | | | | |
|-------|---|---|---|---|---|---|

| Mental State | Exit Condition |
|--------------|----------------|

| Notes: |
|--------|

| Satoshis W/L | | % of acct | | USD Value | |
|--------------|---|-----------|---|-----------|---|

| Buy | Sell | Date Time | | Date Time | | Outcome |
|-----|------|-----------|---|-----------|---|---------|
| Pair | | Entry Price | | Exit Price | | Profit / Loss |

| Setup | | | | | | |
|-------|---|---|---|---|---|---|

| Mental State | Exit Condition |
|--------------|----------------|

| Notes: |
|--------|

| Satoshis W/L | | % of acct | | USD Value | |
|--------------|---|-----------|---|-----------|---|

# CRYPTO CURRENCY TRADING TRACKER

| Buy | Sell | Date Time | | Date Time | | Outcome |
|-----|------|-----------|--|-----------|--|---------|
| Pair | | Entry Price | | Exit Price | | Profit / Loss |

| Setup |
|-------|

| Mental State | Exit Condition |
|--------------|----------------|

| Notes: |
|--------|

| Satoshis W/L | | % of acct | | USD Value | |
|--------------|--|-----------|--|-----------|--|

| Buy | Sell | Date Time | | Date Time | | Outcome |
|-----|------|-----------|--|-----------|--|---------|
| Pair | | Entry Price | | Exit Price | | Profit / Loss |

| Setup |
|-------|

| Mental State | Exit Condition |
|--------------|----------------|

| Notes: |
|--------|

| Satoshis W/L | | % of acct | | USD Value | |
|--------------|--|-----------|--|-----------|--|

| Buy | Sell | Date Time | | Date Time | | Outcome |
|-----|------|-----------|--|-----------|--|---------|
| Pair | | Entry Price | | Exit Price | | Profit / Loss |

| Setup |
|-------|

| Mental State | Exit Condition |
|--------------|----------------|

| Notes: |
|--------|

| Satoshis W/L | | % of acct | | USD Value | |
|--------------|--|-----------|--|-----------|--|

# CRYPTO CURRENCY TRADING TRACKER

| Buy | Sell | Date Time | | Date Time | | Outcome |
|-----|------|-----------|---|-----------|---|---------|
| Pair | | Entry Price | | Exit Price | | Profit / Loss |

**Setup**

| Mental State | Exit Condition |
|--------------|----------------|

**Notes:**

| Satoshis W/L | | % of acct | | USD Value | |
|--------------|---|-----------|---|-----------|---|

| Buy | Sell | Date Time | | Date Time | | Outcome |
|-----|------|-----------|---|-----------|---|---------|
| Pair | | Entry Price | | Exit Price | | Profit / Loss |

**Setup**

| Mental State | Exit Condition |
|--------------|----------------|

**Notes:**

| Satoshis W/L | | % of acct | | USD Value | |
|--------------|---|-----------|---|-----------|---|

| Buy | Sell | Date Time | | Date Time | | Outcome |
|-----|------|-----------|---|-----------|---|---------|
| Pair | | Entry Price | | Exit Price | | Profit / Loss |

**Setup**

| Mental State | Exit Condition |
|--------------|----------------|

**Notes:**

| Satoshis W/L | | % of acct | | USD Value | |
|--------------|---|-----------|---|-----------|---|

# CRYPTO CURRENCY TRADING TRACKER

| Buy | Sell | Date Time | | Date Time | | Outcome |
|-----|------|-----------|---|-----------|---|---------|
| Pair | | Entry Price | | Exit Price | | Profit / Loss |
| Setup | | | | | | |
| Mental State | | | Exit Condition | | | |
| Notes: | | | | | | |
| Satoshis W/L | | | % of acct | | USD Value | |

| Buy | Sell | Date Time | | Date Time | | Outcome |
|-----|------|-----------|---|-----------|---|---------|
| Pair | | Entry Price | | Exit Price | | Profit / Loss |
| Setup | | | | | | |
| Mental State | | | Exit Condition | | | |
| Notes: | | | | | | |
| Satoshis W/L | | | % of acct | | USD Value | |

| Buy | Sell | Date Time | | Date Time | | Outcome |
|-----|------|-----------|---|-----------|---|---------|
| Pair | | Entry Price | | Exit Price | | Profit / Loss |
| Setup | | | | | | |
| Mental State | | | Exit Condition | | | |
| Notes: | | | | | | |
| Satoshis W/L | | | % of acct | | USD Value | |

# CRYPTO CURRENCY TRADING TRACKER

| Buy | Sell | Date Time | | Date Time | | Outcome |
|---|---|---|---|---|---|---|
| Pair | | Entry Price | | Exit Price | | Profit / Loss |

**Setup**

| Mental State | Exit Condition |
|---|---|
| | |

**Notes:**

| Satoshis W/L | | % of acct | | USD Value | |
|---|---|---|---|---|---|

| Buy | Sell | Date Time | | Date Time | | Outcome |
|---|---|---|---|---|---|---|
| Pair | | Entry Price | | Exit Price | | Profit / Loss |

**Setup**

| Mental State | Exit Condition |
|---|---|
| | |

**Notes:**

| Satoshis W/L | | % of acct | | USD Value | |
|---|---|---|---|---|---|

| Buy | Sell | Date Time | | Date Time | | Outcome |
|---|---|---|---|---|---|---|
| Pair | | Entry Price | | Exit Price | | Profit / Loss |

**Setup**

| Mental State | Exit Condition |
|---|---|
| | |

**Notes:**

| Satoshis W/L | | % of acct | | USD Value | |
|---|---|---|---|---|---|

# CRYPTO CURRENCY TRADING TRACKER

| Buy | Sell | Date Time | | Date Time | | Outcome |
|---|---|---|---|---|---|---|
| Pair | | Entry Price | | Exit Price | | Profit / Loss |

| Setup | | | | | | |
|---|---|---|---|---|---|---|

| Mental State | | | Exit Condition | | | |
|---|---|---|---|---|---|---|

| Notes: | | | | | | |
|---|---|---|---|---|---|---|

| Satoshis W/L | | | % of acct | | USD Value | |
|---|---|---|---|---|---|---|

| Buy | Sell | Date Time | | Date Time | | Outcome |
|---|---|---|---|---|---|---|
| Pair | | Entry Price | | Exit Price | | Profit / Loss |

| Setup | | | | | | |
|---|---|---|---|---|---|---|

| Mental State | | | Exit Condition | | | |
|---|---|---|---|---|---|---|

| Notes: | | | | | | |
|---|---|---|---|---|---|---|

| Satoshis W/L | | | % of acct | | USD Value | |
|---|---|---|---|---|---|---|

| Buy | Sell | Date Time | | Date Time | | Outcome |
|---|---|---|---|---|---|---|
| Pair | | Entry Price | | Exit Price | | Profit / Loss |

| Setup | | | | | | |
|---|---|---|---|---|---|---|

| Mental State | | | Exit Condition | | | |
|---|---|---|---|---|---|---|

| Notes: | | | | | | |
|---|---|---|---|---|---|---|

| Satoshis W/L | | | % of acct | | USD Value | |
|---|---|---|---|---|---|---|

# CRYPTO CURRENCY TRADING TRACKER

| Buy | Sell | Date Time | | Date Time | | Outcome |
|---|---|---|---|---|---|---|
| Pair | | Entry Price | | Exit Price | | Profit / Loss |

**Setup**

| Mental State | Exit Condition |
|---|---|
| | |

**Notes:**

| Satoshis W/L | | % of acct | | USD Value | |
|---|---|---|---|---|---|

| Buy | Sell | Date Time | | Date Time | | Outcome |
|---|---|---|---|---|---|---|
| Pair | | Entry Price | | Exit Price | | Profit / Loss |

**Setup**

| Mental State | Exit Condition |
|---|---|
| | |

**Notes:**

| Satoshis W/L | | % of acct | | USD Value | |
|---|---|---|---|---|---|

| Buy | Sell | Date Time | | Date Time | | Outcome |
|---|---|---|---|---|---|---|
| Pair | | Entry Price | | Exit Price | | Profit / Loss |

**Setup**

| Mental State | Exit Condition |
|---|---|
| | |

**Notes:**

| Satoshis W/L | | % of acct | | USD Value | |
|---|---|---|---|---|---|

# CRYPTO CURRENCY TRADING TRACKER

| Buy | Sell | Date Time | | Date Time | | Outcome |
|---|---|---|---|---|---|---|
| Pair | | Entry Price | | Exit Price | | Profit / Loss |

| Setup |
|---|

| Mental State | Exit Condition |
|---|---|

| Notes: |
|---|

| Satoshis W/L | | % of acct | | USD Value | |
|---|---|---|---|---|---|

| Buy | Sell | Date Time | | Date Time | | Outcome |
|---|---|---|---|---|---|---|
| Pair | | Entry Price | | Exit Price | | Profit / Loss |

| Setup |
|---|

| Mental State | Exit Condition |
|---|---|

| Notes: |
|---|

| Satoshis W/L | | % of acct | | USD Value | |
|---|---|---|---|---|---|

| Buy | Sell | Date Time | | Date Time | | Outcome |
|---|---|---|---|---|---|---|
| Pair | | Entry Price | | Exit Price | | Profit / Loss |

| Setup |
|---|

| Mental State | Exit Condition |
|---|---|

| Notes: |
|---|

| Satoshis W/L | | % of acct | | USD Value | |
|---|---|---|---|---|---|

# CRYPTO CURRENCY TRADING TRACKER

| Buy | Sell | Date Time | | Date Time | | Outcome |
|-----|------|-----------|--|-----------|--|---------|
| Pair | | Entry Price | | Exit Price | | Profit / Loss |

| Setup | | | | | | |
|-------|--|--|--|--|--|--|

| Mental State | | | Exit Condition | | | |
|--------------|--|--|----------------|--|--|--|

| Notes: | | | | | | |
|--------|--|--|--|--|--|--|

| Satoshis W/L | | % of acct | | USD Value | |
|--------------|--|-----------|--|-----------|--|

| Buy | Sell | Date Time | | Date Time | | Outcome |
|-----|------|-----------|--|-----------|--|---------|
| Pair | | Entry Price | | Exit Price | | Profit / Loss |

| Setup | | | | | | |
|-------|--|--|--|--|--|--|

| Mental State | | | Exit Condition | | | |
|--------------|--|--|----------------|--|--|--|

| Notes: | | | | | | |
|--------|--|--|--|--|--|--|

| Satoshis W/L | | % of acct | | USD Value | |
|--------------|--|-----------|--|-----------|--|

| Buy | Sell | Date Time | | Date Time | | Outcome |
|-----|------|-----------|--|-----------|--|---------|
| Pair | | Entry Price | | Exit Price | | Profit / Loss |

| Setup | | | | | | |
|-------|--|--|--|--|--|--|

| Mental State | | | Exit Condition | | | |
|--------------|--|--|----------------|--|--|--|

| Notes: | | | | | | |
|--------|--|--|--|--|--|--|

| Satoshis W/L | | % of acct | | USD Value | |
|--------------|--|-----------|--|-----------|--|

# CRYPTO CURRENCY TRADING TRACKER

| Buy | Sell | Date Time | | Date Time | | Outcome |
|---|---|---|---|---|---|---|
| Pair | | Entry Price | | Exit Price | | Profit / Loss |

| Setup | | | | | | |
|---|---|---|---|---|---|---|
| Mental State | | | Exit Condition | | | |
| Notes: | | | | | | |
| Satoshis W/L | | % of acct | | USD Value | | |

| Buy | Sell | Date Time | | Date Time | | Outcome |
|---|---|---|---|---|---|---|
| Pair | | Entry Price | | Exit Price | | Profit / Loss |

| Setup | | | | | | |
|---|---|---|---|---|---|---|
| Mental State | | | Exit Condition | | | |
| Notes: | | | | | | |
| Satoshis W/L | | % of acct | | USD Value | | |

| Buy | Sell | Date Time | | Date Time | | Outcome |
|---|---|---|---|---|---|---|
| Pair | | Entry Price | | Exit Price | | Profit / Loss |

| Setup | | | | | | |
|---|---|---|---|---|---|---|
| Mental State | | | Exit Condition | | | |
| Notes: | | | | | | |
| Satoshis W/L | | % of acct | | USD Value | | |

# CRYPTO CURRENCY TRADING TRACKER

| Buy | Sell | Date Time | | Date Time | | Outcome |
|---|---|---|---|---|---|---|
| Pair | | Entry Price | | Exit Price | | Profit / Loss |

| Setup | | | | | | |
|---|---|---|---|---|---|---|

| Mental State | | | Exit Condition | | | |
|---|---|---|---|---|---|---|

| Notes: | | | | | | |
|---|---|---|---|---|---|---|

| Satoshis W/L | | % of acct | | USD Value | |
|---|---|---|---|---|---|

| Buy | Sell | Date Time | | Date Time | | Outcome |
|---|---|---|---|---|---|---|
| Pair | | Entry Price | | Exit Price | | Profit / Loss |

| Setup | | | | | | |
|---|---|---|---|---|---|---|

| Mental State | | | Exit Condition | | | |
|---|---|---|---|---|---|---|

| Notes: | | | | | | |
|---|---|---|---|---|---|---|

| Satoshis W/L | | % of acct | | USD Value | |
|---|---|---|---|---|---|

| Buy | Sell | Date Time | | Date Time | | Outcome |
|---|---|---|---|---|---|---|
| Pair | | Entry Price | | Exit Price | | Profit / Loss |

| Setup | | | | | | |
|---|---|---|---|---|---|---|

| Mental State | | | Exit Condition | | | |
|---|---|---|---|---|---|---|

| Notes: | | | | | | |
|---|---|---|---|---|---|---|

| Satoshis W/L | | % of acct | | USD Value | |
|---|---|---|---|---|---|

# CRYPTO CURRENCY TRADING TRACKER

| Buy | Sell | Date Time | | Date Time | | Outcome |
|-----|------|-----------|---|-----------|---|---------|
| Pair | | Entry Price | | Exit Price | | Profit / Loss |
| Setup | | | | | | |
| Mental State | | | Exit Condition | | | |
| Notes: | | | | | | |
| Satoshis W/L | | | % of acct | | USD Value | |

| Buy | Sell | Date Time | | Date Time | | Outcome |
|-----|------|-----------|---|-----------|---|---------|
| Pair | | Entry Price | | Exit Price | | Profit / Loss |
| Setup | | | | | | |
| Mental State | | | Exit Condition | | | |
| Notes: | | | | | | |
| Satoshis W/L | | | % of acct | | USD Value | |

| Buy | Sell | Date Time | | Date Time | | Outcome |
|-----|------|-----------|---|-----------|---|---------|
| Pair | | Entry Price | | Exit Price | | Profit / Loss |
| Setup | | | | | | |
| Mental State | | | Exit Condition | | | |
| Notes: | | | | | | |
| Satoshis W/L | | | % of acct | | USD Value | |

# CRYPTO CURRENCY TRADING TRACKER

| Buy | Sell | Date Time | | Date Time | | Outcome |
|-----|------|-----------|---|-----------|---|---------|
| Pair | | Entry Price | | Exit Price | | Profit / Loss |

Setup

| Mental State | | Exit Condition | |

Notes:

| Satoshis W/L | | % of acct | | USD Value | |

| Buy | Sell | Date Time | | Date Time | | Outcome |
|-----|------|-----------|---|-----------|---|---------|
| Pair | | Entry Price | | Exit Price | | Profit / Loss |

Setup

| Mental State | | Exit Condition | |

Notes:

| Satoshis W/L | | % of acct | | USD Value | |

| Buy | Sell | Date Time | | Date Time | | Outcome |
|-----|------|-----------|---|-----------|---|---------|
| Pair | | Entry Price | | Exit Price | | Profit / Loss |

Setup

| Mental State | | Exit Condition | |

Notes:

| Satoshis W/L | | % of acct | | USD Value | |

# CRYPTO CURRENCY TRADING TRACKER

| Buy | Sell | Date Time | | Date Time | | Outcome |
|-----|------|-----------|---|-----------|---|---------|
| Pair | | Entry Price | | Exit Price | | Profit / Loss |

**Setup**

| Mental State | Exit Condition |
|--------------|----------------|
| | |

**Notes:**

| Satoshis W/L | | % of acct | | USD Value | |
|--------------|---|-----------|---|-----------|---|

| Buy | Sell | Date Time | | Date Time | | Outcome |
|-----|------|-----------|---|-----------|---|---------|
| Pair | | Entry Price | | Exit Price | | Profit / Loss |

**Setup**

| Mental State | Exit Condition |
|--------------|----------------|
| | |

**Notes:**

| Satoshis W/L | | % of acct | | USD Value | |
|--------------|---|-----------|---|-----------|---|

| Buy | Sell | Date Time | | Date Time | | Outcome |
|-----|------|-----------|---|-----------|---|---------|
| Pair | | Entry Price | | Exit Price | | Profit / Loss |

**Setup**

| Mental State | Exit Condition |
|--------------|----------------|
| | |

**Notes:**

| Satoshis W/L | | % of acct | | USD Value | |
|--------------|---|-----------|---|-----------|---|

# CRYPTO CURRENCY TRADING TRACKER

| Buy | Sell | Date Time | | Date Time | | Outcome |
|---|---|---|---|---|---|---|
| Pair | | Entry Price | | Exit Price | | Profit / Loss |

| Setup | | | | | | |
|---|---|---|---|---|---|---|

| Mental State | | | Exit Condition | | | |
|---|---|---|---|---|---|---|

| Notes: | | | | | | |
|---|---|---|---|---|---|---|

| Satoshis W/L | | % of acct | | USD Value | |
|---|---|---|---|---|---|

| Buy | Sell | Date Time | | Date Time | | Outcome |
|---|---|---|---|---|---|---|
| Pair | | Entry Price | | Exit Price | | Profit / Loss |

| Setup | | | | | | |
|---|---|---|---|---|---|---|

| Mental State | | | Exit Condition | | | |
|---|---|---|---|---|---|---|

| Notes: | | | | | | |
|---|---|---|---|---|---|---|

| Satoshis W/L | | % of acct | | USD Value | |
|---|---|---|---|---|---|

| Buy | Sell | Date Time | | Date Time | | Outcome |
|---|---|---|---|---|---|---|
| Pair | | Entry Price | | Exit Price | | Profit / Loss |

| Setup | | | | | | |
|---|---|---|---|---|---|---|

| Mental State | | | Exit Condition | | | |
|---|---|---|---|---|---|---|

| Notes: | | | | | | |
|---|---|---|---|---|---|---|

| Satoshis W/L | | % of acct | | USD Value | |
|---|---|---|---|---|---|

# CRYPTO CURRENCY TRADING TRACKER

| Buy | Sell | Date Time | | Date Time | | Outcome |
|-----|------|-----------|--|-----------|--|---------|
| Pair | | Entry Price | | Exit Price | | Profit / Loss |

| Setup |
|-------|
| |

| Mental State | Exit Condition |
|--------------|----------------|
| | |

| Notes: |
|--------|
| |

| Satoshis W/L | | % of acct | | USD Value | |
|--------------|--|-----------|--|-----------|--|

| Buy | Sell | Date Time | | Date Time | | Outcome |
|-----|------|-----------|--|-----------|--|---------|
| Pair | | Entry Price | | Exit Price | | Profit / Loss |

| Setup |
|-------|
| |

| Mental State | Exit Condition |
|--------------|----------------|
| | |

| Notes: |
|--------|
| |

| Satoshis W/L | | % of acct | | USD Value | |
|--------------|--|-----------|--|-----------|--|

| Buy | Sell | Date Time | | Date Time | | Outcome |
|-----|------|-----------|--|-----------|--|---------|
| Pair | | Entry Price | | Exit Price | | Profit / Loss |

| Setup |
|-------|
| |

| Mental State | Exit Condition |
|--------------|----------------|
| | |

| Notes: |
|--------|
| |

| Satoshis W/L | | % of acct | | USD Value | |
|--------------|--|-----------|--|-----------|--|

# CRYPTO CURRENCY TRADING TRACKER

| Buy | Sell | Date Time | | Date Time | | Outcome |
|-----|------|-----------|---|-----------|---|---------|
| Pair | | Entry Price | | Exit Price | | Profit / Loss |

**Setup**

| Mental State | Exit Condition |
|--------------|----------------|
| | |

**Notes:**

| Satoshis W/L | | % of acct | | USD Value | |
|--------------|---|-----------|---|-----------|---|

| Buy | Sell | Date Time | | Date Time | | Outcome |
|-----|------|-----------|---|-----------|---|---------|
| Pair | | Entry Price | | Exit Price | | Profit / Loss |

**Setup**

| Mental State | Exit Condition |
|--------------|----------------|
| | |

**Notes:**

| Satoshis W/L | | % of acct | | USD Value | |
|--------------|---|-----------|---|-----------|---|

| Buy | Sell | Date Time | | Date Time | | Outcome |
|-----|------|-----------|---|-----------|---|---------|
| Pair | | Entry Price | | Exit Price | | Profit / Loss |

**Setup**

| Mental State | Exit Condition |
|--------------|----------------|
| | |

**Notes:**

| Satoshis W/L | | % of acct | | USD Value | |
|--------------|---|-----------|---|-----------|---|

# CRYPTO CURRENCY TRADING TRACKER

| Buy | Sell | Date Time | | Date Time | | Outcome |
|---|---|---|---|---|---|---|
| Pair | | Entry Price | | Exit Price | | Profit / Loss |

| Setup | | | | | | |
|---|---|---|---|---|---|---|

| Mental State | | Exit Condition | |
|---|---|---|---|

| Notes: | | | | |
|---|---|---|---|---|

| Satoshis W/L | | % of acct | | USD Value | |
|---|---|---|---|---|---|

| Buy | Sell | Date Time | | Date Time | | Outcome |
|---|---|---|---|---|---|---|
| Pair | | Entry Price | | Exit Price | | Profit / Loss |

| Setup | | | | | | |
|---|---|---|---|---|---|---|

| Mental State | | Exit Condition | |
|---|---|---|---|

| Notes: | | | | |
|---|---|---|---|---|

| Satoshis W/L | | % of acct | | USD Value | |
|---|---|---|---|---|---|

| Buy | Sell | Date Time | | Date Time | | Outcome |
|---|---|---|---|---|---|---|
| Pair | | Entry Price | | Exit Price | | Profit / Loss |

| Setup | | | | | | |
|---|---|---|---|---|---|---|

| Mental State | | Exit Condition | |
|---|---|---|---|

| Notes: | | | | |
|---|---|---|---|---|

| Satoshis W/L | | % of acct | | USD Value | |
|---|---|---|---|---|---|

# CRYPTO CURRENCY TRADING TRACKER

| Buy | Sell | Date Time | | Date Time | | Outcome |
|---|---|---|---|---|---|---|
| Pair | | Entry Price | | Exit Price | | Profit / Loss |

| Setup |
|---|

| Mental State | Exit Condition |
|---|---|

| Notes: |
|---|

| Satoshis W/L | | % of acct | | USD Value | |
|---|---|---|---|---|---|

| Buy | Sell | Date Time | | Date Time | | Outcome |
|---|---|---|---|---|---|---|
| Pair | | Entry Price | | Exit Price | | Profit / Loss |

| Setup |
|---|

| Mental State | Exit Condition |
|---|---|

| Notes: |
|---|

| Satoshis W/L | | % of acct | | USD Value | |
|---|---|---|---|---|---|

| Buy | Sell | Date Time | | Date Time | | Outcome |
|---|---|---|---|---|---|---|
| Pair | | Entry Price | | Exit Price | | Profit / Loss |

| Setup |
|---|

| Mental State | Exit Condition |
|---|---|

| Notes: |
|---|

| Satoshis W/L | | % of acct | | USD Value | |
|---|---|---|---|---|---|

# CRYPTO CURRENCY TRADING TRACKER

| Buy | Sell | Date Time | | Date Time | | Outcome |
|-----|------|-----------|---|-----------|---|---------|
| Pair | | Entry Price | | Exit Price | | Profit / Loss |

Setup

| Mental State | Exit Condition |
|--------------|----------------|

Notes:

| Satoshis W/L | | % of acct | | USD Value | |
|--------------|---|-----------|---|-----------|---|

| Buy | Sell | Date Time | | Date Time | | Outcome |
|-----|------|-----------|---|-----------|---|---------|
| Pair | | Entry Price | | Exit Price | | Profit / Loss |

Setup

| Mental State | Exit Condition |
|--------------|----------------|

Notes:

| Satoshis W/L | | % of acct | | USD Value | |
|--------------|---|-----------|---|-----------|---|

| Buy | Sell | Date Time | | Date Time | | Outcome |
|-----|------|-----------|---|-----------|---|---------|
| Pair | | Entry Price | | Exit Price | | Profit / Loss |

Setup

| Mental State | Exit Condition |
|--------------|----------------|

Notes:

| Satoshis W/L | | % of acct | | USD Value | |
|--------------|---|-----------|---|-----------|---|

# CRYPTO CURRENCY TRADING TRACKER

| Buy | Sell | Date Time | | Date Time | | Outcome |
|---|---|---|---|---|---|---|
| Pair | | Entry Price | | Exit Price | | Profit / Loss |

**Setup**

| Mental State | | Exit Condition | |
|---|---|---|---|

**Notes:**

| Satoshis W/L | | % of acct | | USD Value | |
|---|---|---|---|---|---|

| Buy | Sell | Date Time | | Date Time | | Outcome |
|---|---|---|---|---|---|---|
| Pair | | Entry Price | | Exit Price | | Profit / Loss |

**Setup**

| Mental State | | Exit Condition | |
|---|---|---|---|

**Notes:**

| Satoshis W/L | | % of acct | | USD Value | |
|---|---|---|---|---|---|

| Buy | Sell | Date Time | | Date Time | | Outcome |
|---|---|---|---|---|---|---|
| Pair | | Entry Price | | Exit Price | | Profit / Loss |

**Setup**

| Mental State | | Exit Condition | |
|---|---|---|---|

**Notes:**

| Satoshis W/L | | % of acct | | USD Value | |
|---|---|---|---|---|---|

# CRYPTO CURRENCY TRADING TRACKER

| Buy | Sell | Date Time | | Date Time | | Outcome |
|-----|------|-----------|--|-----------|--|---------|
| Pair | | Entry Price | | Exit Price | | Profit / Loss |

Setup

| Mental State | Exit Condition |
|--------------|----------------|
| | |

Notes:

| Satoshis W/L | | % of acct | | USD Value | |
|--------------|--|-----------|--|-----------|--|

| Buy | Sell | Date Time | | Date Time | | Outcome |
|-----|------|-----------|--|-----------|--|---------|
| Pair | | Entry Price | | Exit Price | | Profit / Loss |

Setup

| Mental State | Exit Condition |
|--------------|----------------|
| | |

Notes:

| Satoshis W/L | | % of acct | | USD Value | |
|--------------|--|-----------|--|-----------|--|

| Buy | Sell | Date Time | | Date Time | | Outcome |
|-----|------|-----------|--|-----------|--|---------|
| Pair | | Entry Price | | Exit Price | | Profit / Loss |

Setup

| Mental State | Exit Condition |
|--------------|----------------|
| | |

Notes:

| Satoshis W/L | | % of acct | | USD Value | |
|--------------|--|-----------|--|-----------|--|

# CRYPTO CURRENCY TRADING TRACKER

| Buy | Sell | Date Time | | Date Time | | Outcome |
|-----|------|-----------|---|-----------|---|---------|
| Pair | | Entry Price | | Exit Price | | Profit / Loss |

**Setup**

| Mental State | Exit Condition |
|---|---|
| | |

**Notes:**

| Satoshis W/L | | % of acct | | USD Value | |
|---|---|---|---|---|---|

| Buy | Sell | Date Time | | Date Time | | Outcome |
|-----|------|-----------|---|-----------|---|---------|
| Pair | | Entry Price | | Exit Price | | Profit / Loss |

**Setup**

| Mental State | Exit Condition |
|---|---|
| | |

**Notes:**

| Satoshis W/L | | % of acct | | USD Value | |
|---|---|---|---|---|---|

| Buy | Sell | Date Time | | Date Time | | Outcome |
|-----|------|-----------|---|-----------|---|---------|
| Pair | | Entry Price | | Exit Price | | Profit / Loss |

**Setup**

| Mental State | Exit Condition |
|---|---|
| | |

**Notes:**

| Satoshis W/L | | % of acct | | USD Value | |
|---|---|---|---|---|---|

# CRYPTO CURRENCY TRADING TRACKER

| Buy | Sell | Date Time | | Date Time | | Outcome |
|-----|------|-----------|--|-----------|--|---------|
| Pair | | Entry Price | | Exit Price | | Profit / Loss |

Setup

| Mental State | Exit Condition |
|--------------|----------------|
| | |

Notes:

| Satoshis W/L | | % of acct | | USD Value | |
|--------------|--|-----------|--|-----------|--|

| Buy | Sell | Date Time | | Date Time | | Outcome |
|-----|------|-----------|--|-----------|--|---------|
| Pair | | Entry Price | | Exit Price | | Profit / Loss |

Setup

| Mental State | Exit Condition |
|--------------|----------------|
| | |

Notes:

| Satoshis W/L | | % of acct | | USD Value | |
|--------------|--|-----------|--|-----------|--|

| Buy | Sell | Date Time | | Date Time | | Outcome |
|-----|------|-----------|--|-----------|--|---------|
| Pair | | Entry Price | | Exit Price | | Profit / Loss |

Setup

| Mental State | Exit Condition |
|--------------|----------------|
| | |

Notes:

| Satoshis W/L | | % of acct | | USD Value | |
|--------------|--|-----------|--|-----------|--|

# CRYPTO CURRENCY TRADING TRACKER

| Buy | Sell | Date Time | | Date Time | | Outcome |
|-----|------|-----------|--|-----------|--|---------|
| Pair | | Entry Price | | Exit Price | | Profit / Loss |

**Setup**

| Mental State | Exit Condition |
|--------------|----------------|

**Notes:**

| Satoshis W/L | | % of acct | | USD Value | |
|--------------|--|-----------|--|-----------|--|

| Buy | Sell | Date Time | | Date Time | | Outcome |
|-----|------|-----------|--|-----------|--|---------|
| Pair | | Entry Price | | Exit Price | | Profit / Loss |

**Setup**

| Mental State | Exit Condition |
|--------------|----------------|

**Notes:**

| Satoshis W/L | | % of acct | | USD Value | |
|--------------|--|-----------|--|-----------|--|

| Buy | Sell | Date Time | | Date Time | | Outcome |
|-----|------|-----------|--|-----------|--|---------|
| Pair | | Entry Price | | Exit Price | | Profit / Loss |

**Setup**

| Mental State | Exit Condition |
|--------------|----------------|

**Notes:**

| Satoshis W/L | | % of acct | | USD Value | |
|--------------|--|-----------|--|-----------|--|

# CRYPTO CURRENCY TRADING TRACKER

| Buy | Sell | Date Time | | Date Time | | Outcome |
|---|---|---|---|---|---|---|
| Pair | | Entry Price | | Exit Price | | Profit / Loss |

**Setup**

| Mental State | Exit Condition |
|---|---|
| | |

**Notes:**

| Satoshis W/L | | % of acct | | USD Value | |
|---|---|---|---|---|---|

| Buy | Sell | Date Time | | Date Time | | Outcome |
|---|---|---|---|---|---|---|
| Pair | | Entry Price | | Exit Price | | Profit / Loss |

**Setup**

| Mental State | Exit Condition |
|---|---|
| | |

**Notes:**

| Satoshis W/L | | % of acct | | USD Value | |
|---|---|---|---|---|---|

| Buy | Sell | Date Time | | Date Time | | Outcome |
|---|---|---|---|---|---|---|
| Pair | | Entry Price | | Exit Price | | Profit / Loss |

**Setup**

| Mental State | Exit Condition |
|---|---|
| | |

**Notes:**

| Satoshis W/L | | % of acct | | USD Value | |
|---|---|---|---|---|---|

# CRYPTO CURRENCY TRADING TRACKER

| Buy | Sell | Date Time | | Date Time | | Outcome | |
|---|---|---|---|---|---|---|---|
| Pair | | Entry Price | | Exit Price | | Profit / Loss | |

**Setup**

| Mental State | Exit Condition |
|---|---|
| | |

**Notes:**

| Satoshis W/L | | % of acct | | USD Value | |
|---|---|---|---|---|---|

| Buy | Sell | Date Time | | Date Time | | Outcome | |
|---|---|---|---|---|---|---|---|
| Pair | | Entry Price | | Exit Price | | Profit / Loss | |

**Setup**

| Mental State | Exit Condition |
|---|---|
| | |

**Notes:**

| Satoshis W/L | | % of acct | | USD Value | |
|---|---|---|---|---|---|

| Buy | Sell | Date Time | | Date Time | | Outcome | |
|---|---|---|---|---|---|---|---|
| Pair | | Entry Price | | Exit Price | | Profit / Loss | |

**Setup**

| Mental State | Exit Condition |
|---|---|
| | |

**Notes:**

| Satoshis W/L | | % of acct | | USD Value | |
|---|---|---|---|---|---|

# CRYPTO CURRENCY TRADING TRACKER

| Buy | Sell | Date Time | | Date Time | | Outcome |
|---|---|---|---|---|---|---|
| Pair | | Entry Price | | Exit Price | | Profit / Loss |

| Setup |
|---|

| Mental State | Exit Condition |
|---|---|

| Notes: |
|---|

| Satoshis W/L | | % of acct | | USD Value | |
|---|---|---|---|---|---|

| Buy | Sell | Date Time | | Date Time | | Outcome |
|---|---|---|---|---|---|---|
| Pair | | Entry Price | | Exit Price | | Profit / Loss |

| Setup |
|---|

| Mental State | Exit Condition |
|---|---|

| Notes: |
|---|

| Satoshis W/L | | % of acct | | USD Value | |
|---|---|---|---|---|---|

| Buy | Sell | Date Time | | Date Time | | Outcome |
|---|---|---|---|---|---|---|
| Pair | | Entry Price | | Exit Price | | Profit / Loss |

| Setup |
|---|

| Mental State | Exit Condition |
|---|---|

| Notes: |
|---|

| Satoshis W/L | | % of acct | | USD Value | |
|---|---|---|---|---|---|

# CRYPTO CURRENCY TRADING TRACKER

| Buy | Sell | Date Time | | Date Time | | Outcome |
|---|---|---|---|---|---|---|
| Pair | | Entry Price | | Exit Price | | Profit / Loss |

| Setup |
|---|

| Mental State | Exit Condition |
|---|---|

| Notes: |
|---|

| Satoshis W/L | | % of acct | | USD Value | |
|---|---|---|---|---|---|

| Buy | Sell | Date Time | | Date Time | | Outcome |
|---|---|---|---|---|---|---|
| Pair | | Entry Price | | Exit Price | | Profit / Loss |

| Setup |
|---|

| Mental State | Exit Condition |
|---|---|

| Notes: |
|---|

| Satoshis W/L | | % of acct | | USD Value | |
|---|---|---|---|---|---|

| Buy | Sell | Date Time | | Date Time | | Outcome |
|---|---|---|---|---|---|---|
| Pair | | Entry Price | | Exit Price | | Profit / Loss |

| Setup |
|---|

| Mental State | Exit Condition |
|---|---|

| Notes: |
|---|

| Satoshis W/L | | % of acct | | USD Value | |
|---|---|---|---|---|---|

# CRYPTO CURRENCY TRADING TRACKER

| Buy | Sell | Date Time | | Date Time | | Outcome |
|-----|------|-----------|---|-----------|---|---------|
| Pair | | Entry Price | | Exit Price | | Profit / Loss |

**Setup**

| Mental State | Exit Condition |
|--------------|----------------|

**Notes:**

| Satoshis W/L | | % of acct | | USD Value | |
|--------------|---|-----------|---|-----------|---|

| Buy | Sell | Date Time | | Date Time | | Outcome |
|-----|------|-----------|---|-----------|---|---------|
| Pair | | Entry Price | | Exit Price | | Profit / Loss |

**Setup**

| Mental State | Exit Condition |
|--------------|----------------|

**Notes:**

| Satoshis W/L | | % of acct | | USD Value | |
|--------------|---|-----------|---|-----------|---|

| Buy | Sell | Date Time | | Date Time | | Outcome |
|-----|------|-----------|---|-----------|---|---------|
| Pair | | Entry Price | | Exit Price | | Profit / Loss |

**Setup**

| Mental State | Exit Condition |
|--------------|----------------|

**Notes:**

| Satoshis W/L | | % of acct | | USD Value | |
|--------------|---|-----------|---|-----------|---|

# CRYPTO CURRENCY TRADING TRACKER

| Buy | Sell | Date Time | | Date Time | | Outcome |
|-----|------|-----------|---|-----------|---|---------|
| Pair | | Entry Price | | Exit Price | | Profit / Loss |

Setup

| Mental State | | Exit Condition | |

Notes:

| Satoshis W/L | | % of acct | | USD Value | |

| Buy | Sell | Date Time | | Date Time | | Outcome |
|-----|------|-----------|---|-----------|---|---------|
| Pair | | Entry Price | | Exit Price | | Profit / Loss |

Setup

| Mental State | | Exit Condition | |

Notes:

| Satoshis W/L | | % of acct | | USD Value | |

| Buy | Sell | Date Time | | Date Time | | Outcome |
|-----|------|-----------|---|-----------|---|---------|
| Pair | | Entry Price | | Exit Price | | Profit / Loss |

Setup

| Mental State | | Exit Condition | |

Notes:

| Satoshis W/L | | % of acct | | USD Value | |

# CRYPTO CURRENCY TRADING TRACKER

| Buy | Sell | Date Time | | Date Time | | Outcome |
|-----|------|-----------|---|-----------|---|---------|
| Pair | | Entry Price | | Exit Price | | Profit / Loss |

**Setup**

| Mental State | Exit Condition |
|--------------|----------------|
| | |

**Notes:**

| Satoshis W/L | | % of acct | | USD Value | |
|--------------|---|-----------|---|-----------|---|

| Buy | Sell | Date Time | | Date Time | | Outcome |
|-----|------|-----------|---|-----------|---|---------|
| Pair | | Entry Price | | Exit Price | | Profit / Loss |

**Setup**

| Mental State | Exit Condition |
|--------------|----------------|
| | |

**Notes:**

| Satoshis W/L | | % of acct | | USD Value | |
|--------------|---|-----------|---|-----------|---|

| Buy | Sell | Date Time | | Date Time | | Outcome |
|-----|------|-----------|---|-----------|---|---------|
| Pair | | Entry Price | | Exit Price | | Profit / Loss |

**Setup**

| Mental State | Exit Condition |
|--------------|----------------|
| | |

**Notes:**

| Satoshis W/L | | % of acct | | USD Value | |
|--------------|---|-----------|---|-----------|---|

# CRYPTO CURRENCY TRADING TRACKER

| Buy | Sell | Date Time | | Date Time | | Outcome |
|---|---|---|---|---|---|---|
| Pair | | Entry Price | | Exit Price | | Profit / Loss |

| Setup | | | | | | |
|---|---|---|---|---|---|---|
| Mental State | | | Exit Condition | | | |
| Notes: | | | | | | |
| Satoshis W/L | | % of acct | | USD Value | | |

| Buy | Sell | Date Time | | Date Time | | Outcome |
|---|---|---|---|---|---|---|
| Pair | | Entry Price | | Exit Price | | Profit / Loss |

| Setup | | | | | | |
|---|---|---|---|---|---|---|
| Mental State | | | Exit Condition | | | |
| Notes: | | | | | | |
| Satoshis W/L | | % of acct | | USD Value | | |

| Buy | Sell | Date Time | | Date Time | | Outcome |
|---|---|---|---|---|---|---|
| Pair | | Entry Price | | Exit Price | | Profit / Loss |

| Setup | | | | | | |
|---|---|---|---|---|---|---|
| Mental State | | | Exit Condition | | | |
| Notes: | | | | | | |
| Satoshis W/L | | % of acct | | USD Value | | |

# CRYPTO CURRENCY TRADING TRACKER

| Buy | Sell | Date Time | | Date Time | | Outcome |
|-----|------|-----------|---|-----------|---|---------|
| Pair | | Entry Price | | Exit Price | | Profit / Loss |

| Setup |
|-------|
|  |

| Mental State | Exit Condition |
|--------------|----------------|
|  |  |

| Notes: |
|--------|
|  |

| Satoshis W/L | | % of acct | | USD Value | |
|--------------|---|-----------|---|-----------|---|

| Buy | Sell | Date Time | | Date Time | | Outcome |
|-----|------|-----------|---|-----------|---|---------|
| Pair | | Entry Price | | Exit Price | | Profit / Loss |

| Setup |
|-------|
|  |

| Mental State | Exit Condition |
|--------------|----------------|
|  |  |

| Notes: |
|--------|
|  |

| Satoshis W/L | | % of acct | | USD Value | |
|--------------|---|-----------|---|-----------|---|

| Buy | Sell | Date Time | | Date Time | | Outcome |
|-----|------|-----------|---|-----------|---|---------|
| Pair | | Entry Price | | Exit Price | | Profit / Loss |

| Setup |
|-------|
|  |

| Mental State | Exit Condition |
|--------------|----------------|
|  |  |

| Notes: |
|--------|
|  |

| Satoshis W/L | | % of acct | | USD Value | |
|--------------|---|-----------|---|-----------|---|

# CRYPTO CURRENCY TRADING TRACKER

| Buy | Sell | Date Time | | Date Time | | Outcome |
|-----|------|-----------|---|-----------|---|---------|
| Pair | | Entry Price | | Exit Price | | Profit / Loss |

**Setup**

| Mental State | Exit Condition |
|---|---|
| | |

**Notes:**

| Satoshis W/L | | % of acct | | USD Value | |
|---|---|---|---|---|---|

---

| Buy | Sell | Date Time | | Date Time | | Outcome |
|-----|------|-----------|---|-----------|---|---------|
| Pair | | Entry Price | | Exit Price | | Profit / Loss |

**Setup**

| Mental State | Exit Condition |
|---|---|
| | |

**Notes:**

| Satoshis W/L | | % of acct | | USD Value | |
|---|---|---|---|---|---|

---

| Buy | Sell | Date Time | | Date Time | | Outcome |
|-----|------|-----------|---|-----------|---|---------|
| Pair | | Entry Price | | Exit Price | | Profit / Loss |

**Setup**

| Mental State | Exit Condition |
|---|---|
| | |

**Notes:**

| Satoshis W/L | | % of acct | | USD Value | |
|---|---|---|---|---|---|

# CRYPTO CURRENCY TRADING TRACKER

| Buy | Sell | Date Time | | Date Time | | Outcome |
|-----|------|-----------|--|-----------|--|---------|
| Pair | | Entry Price | | Exit Price | | Profit / Loss |

**Setup**

| Mental State | Exit Condition |
|--------------|----------------|
| | |

**Notes:**

| Satoshis W/L | | % of acct | | USD Value | |
|--------------|--|-----------|--|-----------|--|

| Buy | Sell | Date Time | | Date Time | | Outcome |
|-----|------|-----------|--|-----------|--|---------|
| Pair | | Entry Price | | Exit Price | | Profit / Loss |

**Setup**

| Mental State | Exit Condition |
|--------------|----------------|
| | |

**Notes:**

| Satoshis W/L | | % of acct | | USD Value | |
|--------------|--|-----------|--|-----------|--|

| Buy | Sell | Date Time | | Date Time | | Outcome |
|-----|------|-----------|--|-----------|--|---------|
| Pair | | Entry Price | | Exit Price | | Profit / Loss |

**Setup**

| Mental State | Exit Condition |
|--------------|----------------|
| | |

**Notes:**

| Satoshis W/L | | % of acct | | USD Value | |
|--------------|--|-----------|--|-----------|--|

# CRYPTO CURRENCY TRADING TRACKER

| Buy | Sell | Date Time | | Date Time | | Outcome |
|---|---|---|---|---|---|---|
| Pair | | Entry Price | | Exit Price | | Profit / Loss |

**Setup**

| Mental State | Exit Condition |
|---|---|
| | |

**Notes:**

| Satoshis W/L | | % of acct | | USD Value | |
|---|---|---|---|---|---|

| Buy | Sell | Date Time | | Date Time | | Outcome |
|---|---|---|---|---|---|---|
| Pair | | Entry Price | | Exit Price | | Profit / Loss |

**Setup**

| Mental State | Exit Condition |
|---|---|
| | |

**Notes:**

| Satoshis W/L | | % of acct | | USD Value | |
|---|---|---|---|---|---|

| Buy | Sell | Date Time | | Date Time | | Outcome |
|---|---|---|---|---|---|---|
| Pair | | Entry Price | | Exit Price | | Profit / Loss |

**Setup**

| Mental State | Exit Condition |
|---|---|
| | |

**Notes:**

| Satoshis W/L | | % of acct | | USD Value | |
|---|---|---|---|---|---|

# CRYPTO CURRENCY TRADING TRACKER

| Buy | Sell | Date Time | | Date Time | | Outcome |
|-----|------|-----------|---|-----------|---|---------|
| Pair | | Entry Price | | Exit Price | | Profit / Loss |

Setup

| Mental State | | Exit Condition | |

Notes:

| Satoshis W/L | | % of acct | | USD Value | |

| Buy | Sell | Date Time | | Date Time | | Outcome |
|-----|------|-----------|---|-----------|---|---------|
| Pair | | Entry Price | | Exit Price | | Profit / Loss |

Setup

| Mental State | | Exit Condition | |

Notes:

| Satoshis W/L | | % of acct | | USD Value | |

| Buy | Sell | Date Time | | Date Time | | Outcome |
|-----|------|-----------|---|-----------|---|---------|
| Pair | | Entry Price | | Exit Price | | Profit / Loss |

Setup

| Mental State | | Exit Condition | |

Notes:

| Satoshis W/L | | % of acct | | USD Value | |

# CRYPTO CURRENCY TRADING TRACKER

| Buy | Sell | Date Time | | Date Time | | Outcome |
|-----|------|-----------|---|-----------|---|---------|
| Pair | | Entry Price | | Exit Price | | Profit / Loss |

| Setup |
|-------|
| |

| Mental State | Exit Condition |
|--------------|----------------|
| | |

| Notes: |
|--------|
| |

| Satoshis W/L | | % of acct | | USD Value | |
|--------------|---|-----------|---|-----------|---|

| Buy | Sell | Date Time | | Date Time | | Outcome |
|-----|------|-----------|---|-----------|---|---------|
| Pair | | Entry Price | | Exit Price | | Profit / Loss |

| Setup |
|-------|
| |

| Mental State | Exit Condition |
|--------------|----------------|
| | |

| Notes: |
|--------|
| |

| Satoshis W/L | | % of acct | | USD Value | |
|--------------|---|-----------|---|-----------|---|

| Buy | Sell | Date Time | | Date Time | | Outcome |
|-----|------|-----------|---|-----------|---|---------|
| Pair | | Entry Price | | Exit Price | | Profit / Loss |

| Setup |
|-------|
| |

| Mental State | Exit Condition |
|--------------|----------------|
| | |

| Notes: |
|--------|
| |

| Satoshis W/L | | % of acct | | USD Value | |
|--------------|---|-----------|---|-----------|---|

# CRYPTO CURRENCY TRADING TRACKER

| Buy | Sell | Date Time | | Date Time | | Outcome |
|-----|------|-----------|---|-----------|---|---------|
| Pair | | Entry Price | | Exit Price | | Profit / Loss |

| Setup |
|-------|
| |

| Mental State | Exit Condition |
|--------------|----------------|
| | |

| Notes: |
|--------|
| |

| Satoshis W/L | | % of acct | | USD Value | |
|--------------|---|-----------|---|-----------|---|

| Buy | Sell | Date Time | | Date Time | | Outcome |
|-----|------|-----------|---|-----------|---|---------|
| Pair | | Entry Price | | Exit Price | | Profit / Loss |

| Setup |
|-------|
| |

| Mental State | Exit Condition |
|--------------|----------------|
| | |

| Notes: |
|--------|
| |

| Satoshis W/L | | % of acct | | USD Value | |
|--------------|---|-----------|---|-----------|---|

| Buy | Sell | Date Time | | Date Time | | Outcome |
|-----|------|-----------|---|-----------|---|---------|
| Pair | | Entry Price | | Exit Price | | Profit / Loss |

| Setup |
|-------|
| |

| Mental State | Exit Condition |
|--------------|----------------|
| | |

| Notes: |
|--------|
| |

| Satoshis W/L | | % of acct | | USD Value | |
|--------------|---|-----------|---|-----------|---|

# CRYPTO CURRENCY TRADING TRACKER

| Buy | Sell | Date Time | | Date Time | | Outcome |
|---|---|---|---|---|---|---|
| Pair | | Entry Price | | Exit Price | | Profit / Loss |

**Setup**

| Mental State | Exit Condition |
|---|---|

**Notes:**

| Satoshis W/L | | % of acct | | USD Value | |
|---|---|---|---|---|---|

| Buy | Sell | Date Time | | Date Time | | Outcome |
|---|---|---|---|---|---|---|
| Pair | | Entry Price | | Exit Price | | Profit / Loss |

**Setup**

| Mental State | Exit Condition |
|---|---|

**Notes:**

| Satoshis W/L | | % of acct | | USD Value | |
|---|---|---|---|---|---|

| Buy | Sell | Date Time | | Date Time | | Outcome |
|---|---|---|---|---|---|---|
| Pair | | Entry Price | | Exit Price | | Profit / Loss |

**Setup**

| Mental State | Exit Condition |
|---|---|

**Notes:**

| Satoshis W/L | | % of acct | | USD Value | |
|---|---|---|---|---|---|

# CRYPTO CURRENCY TRADING TRACKER

| Buy | Sell | Date Time | | Date Time | | Outcome |
|---|---|---|---|---|---|---|
| Pair | | Entry Price | | Exit Price | | Profit / Loss |

| Setup |
|---|

| Mental State | Exit Condition |
|---|---|

| Notes: |
|---|

| Satoshis W/L | | % of acct | | USD Value | |
|---|---|---|---|---|---|

| Buy | Sell | Date Time | | Date Time | | Outcome |
|---|---|---|---|---|---|---|
| Pair | | Entry Price | | Exit Price | | Profit / Loss |

| Setup |
|---|

| Mental State | Exit Condition |
|---|---|

| Notes: |
|---|

| Satoshis W/L | | % of acct | | USD Value | |
|---|---|---|---|---|---|

| Buy | Sell | Date Time | | Date Time | | Outcome |
|---|---|---|---|---|---|---|
| Pair | | Entry Price | | Exit Price | | Profit / Loss |

| Setup |
|---|

| Mental State | Exit Condition |
|---|---|

| Notes: |
|---|

| Satoshis W/L | | % of acct | | USD Value | |
|---|---|---|---|---|---|

# CRYPTO CURRENCY TRADING TRACKER

| Buy | Sell | Date Time | | Date Time | | Outcome |
|-----|------|-----------|--|-----------|--|---------|
| Pair | | Entry Price | | Exit Price | | Profit / Loss |

| Setup |
|-------|
|       |

| Mental State | Exit Condition |
|--------------|----------------|
|              |                |

| Notes: |
|--------|
|        |

| Satoshis W/L | | % of acct | | USD Value | |
|--------------|--|-----------|--|-----------|--|

| Buy | Sell | Date Time | | Date Time | | Outcome |
|-----|------|-----------|--|-----------|--|---------|
| Pair | | Entry Price | | Exit Price | | Profit / Loss |

| Setup |
|-------|
|       |

| Mental State | Exit Condition |
|--------------|----------------|
|              |                |

| Notes: |
|--------|
|        |

| Satoshis W/L | | % of acct | | USD Value | |
|--------------|--|-----------|--|-----------|--|

| Buy | Sell | Date Time | | Date Time | | Outcome |
|-----|------|-----------|--|-----------|--|---------|
| Pair | | Entry Price | | Exit Price | | Profit / Loss |

| Setup |
|-------|
|       |

| Mental State | Exit Condition |
|--------------|----------------|
|              |                |

| Notes: |
|--------|
|        |

| Satoshis W/L | | % of acct | | USD Value | |
|--------------|--|-----------|--|-----------|--|

# CRYPTO CURRENCY TRADING TRACKER

| Buy | Sell | Date Time | | Date Time | | Outcome |
|-----|------|-----------|---|-----------|---|---------|
| Pair | | Entry Price | | Exit Price | | Profit / Loss |

**Setup**

| Mental State | Exit Condition |
|--------------|----------------|

**Notes:**

| Satoshis W/L | | % of acct | | USD Value | |
|--------------|---|-----------|---|-----------|---|

| Buy | Sell | Date Time | | Date Time | | Outcome |
|-----|------|-----------|---|-----------|---|---------|
| Pair | | Entry Price | | Exit Price | | Profit / Loss |

**Setup**

| Mental State | Exit Condition |
|--------------|----------------|

**Notes:**

| Satoshis W/L | | % of acct | | USD Value | |
|--------------|---|-----------|---|-----------|---|

| Buy | Sell | Date Time | | Date Time | | Outcome |
|-----|------|-----------|---|-----------|---|---------|
| Pair | | Entry Price | | Exit Price | | Profit / Loss |

**Setup**

| Mental State | Exit Condition |
|--------------|----------------|

**Notes:**

| Satoshis W/L | | % of acct | | USD Value | |
|--------------|---|-----------|---|-----------|---|

# CRYPTO CURRENCY TRADING TRACKER

| Buy | Sell | Date Time | | Date Time | | Outcome |
|-----|------|-----------|--|-----------|--|---------|
| Pair | | Entry Price | | Exit Price | | Profit / Loss |

**Setup**

| Mental State | Exit Condition |
|--------------|----------------|

**Notes:**

| Satoshis W/L | | % of acct | | USD Value | |
|--------------|--|-----------|--|-----------|--|

| Buy | Sell | Date Time | | Date Time | | Outcome |
|-----|------|-----------|--|-----------|--|---------|
| Pair | | Entry Price | | Exit Price | | Profit / Loss |

**Setup**

| Mental State | Exit Condition |
|--------------|----------------|

**Notes:**

| Satoshis W/L | | % of acct | | USD Value | |
|--------------|--|-----------|--|-----------|--|

| Buy | Sell | Date Time | | Date Time | | Outcome |
|-----|------|-----------|--|-----------|--|---------|
| Pair | | Entry Price | | Exit Price | | Profit / Loss |

**Setup**

| Mental State | Exit Condition |
|--------------|----------------|

**Notes:**

| Satoshis W/L | | % of acct | | USD Value | |
|--------------|--|-----------|--|-----------|--|

# CRYPTO CURRENCY TRADING TRACKER

| Buy | Sell | Date Time | | Date Time | | Outcome |
|---|---|---|---|---|---|---|
| Pair | | Entry Price | | Exit Price | | Profit / Loss |

**Setup**

| Mental State | Exit Condition |
|---|---|
| | |

**Notes:**

| Satoshis W/L | | % of acct | | USD Value | |
|---|---|---|---|---|---|

| Buy | Sell | Date Time | | Date Time | | Outcome |
|---|---|---|---|---|---|---|
| Pair | | Entry Price | | Exit Price | | Profit / Loss |

**Setup**

| Mental State | Exit Condition |
|---|---|
| | |

**Notes:**

| Satoshis W/L | | % of acct | | USD Value | |
|---|---|---|---|---|---|

| Buy | Sell | Date Time | | Date Time | | Outcome |
|---|---|---|---|---|---|---|
| Pair | | Entry Price | | Exit Price | | Profit / Loss |

**Setup**

| Mental State | Exit Condition |
|---|---|
| | |

**Notes:**

| Satoshis W/L | | % of acct | | USD Value | |
|---|---|---|---|---|---|

# CRYPTO CURRENCY TRADING TRACKER

| Buy | Sell | Date Time | | Date Time | | Outcome |
|---|---|---|---|---|---|---|
| Pair | | Entry Price | | Exit Price | | Profit / Loss |

**Setup**

| Mental State | Exit Condition |
|---|---|
| | |

**Notes:**

| Satoshis W/L | | % of acct | | USD Value | |
|---|---|---|---|---|---|

| Buy | Sell | Date Time | | Date Time | | Outcome |
|---|---|---|---|---|---|---|
| Pair | | Entry Price | | Exit Price | | Profit / Loss |

**Setup**

| Mental State | Exit Condition |
|---|---|
| | |

**Notes:**

| Satoshis W/L | | % of acct | | USD Value | |
|---|---|---|---|---|---|

| Buy | Sell | Date Time | | Date Time | | Outcome |
|---|---|---|---|---|---|---|
| Pair | | Entry Price | | Exit Price | | Profit / Loss |

**Setup**

| Mental State | Exit Condition |
|---|---|
| | |

**Notes:**

| Satoshis W/L | | % of acct | | USD Value | |
|---|---|---|---|---|---|

# CRYPTO CURRENCY TRADING TRACKER

| Buy | Sell | Date Time | | Date Time | | Outcome |
|---|---|---|---|---|---|---|
| Pair | | Entry Price | | Exit Price | | Profit / Loss |

| Setup |
|---|

| Mental State | Exit Condition |
|---|---|

| Notes: |
|---|

| Satoshis W/L | | % of acct | | USD Value | |
|---|---|---|---|---|---|

| Buy | Sell | Date Time | | Date Time | | Outcome |
|---|---|---|---|---|---|---|
| Pair | | Entry Price | | Exit Price | | Profit / Loss |

| Setup |
|---|

| Mental State | Exit Condition |
|---|---|

| Notes: |
|---|

| Satoshis W/L | | % of acct | | USD Value | |
|---|---|---|---|---|---|

| Buy | Sell | Date Time | | Date Time | | Outcome |
|---|---|---|---|---|---|---|
| Pair | | Entry Price | | Exit Price | | Profit / Loss |

| Setup |
|---|

| Mental State | Exit Condition |
|---|---|

| Notes: |
|---|

| Satoshis W/L | | % of acct | | USD Value | |
|---|---|---|---|---|---|

# CRYPTO CURRENCY TRADING TRACKER

| Buy | Sell | Date Time | | Date Time | | Outcome | |
|-----|------|-----------|---|-----------|---|---------|---|
| Pair | | Entry Price | | Exit Price | | Profit / Loss | |

**Setup**

| Mental State | | Exit Condition | |
|--------------|---|----------------|---|

**Notes:**

| Satoshis W/L | | % of acct | | USD Value | |
|--------------|---|-----------|---|-----------|---|

| Buy | Sell | Date Time | | Date Time | | Outcome | |
|-----|------|-----------|---|-----------|---|---------|---|
| Pair | | Entry Price | | Exit Price | | Profit / Loss | |

**Setup**

| Mental State | | Exit Condition | |
|--------------|---|----------------|---|

**Notes:**

| Satoshis W/L | | % of acct | | USD Value | |
|--------------|---|-----------|---|-----------|---|

| Buy | Sell | Date Time | | Date Time | | Outcome | |
|-----|------|-----------|---|-----------|---|---------|---|
| Pair | | Entry Price | | Exit Price | | Profit / Loss | |

**Setup**

| Mental State | | Exit Condition | |
|--------------|---|----------------|---|

**Notes:**

| Satoshis W/L | | % of acct | | USD Value | |
|--------------|---|-----------|---|-----------|---|

www.ingramcontent.com/pod-product-compliance
Lightning Source LLC
Chambersburg PA
CBHW070846070326
40690CB00009B/1722